FEARLESS™
D!ALOGUES

For more information on Fearless Dialogues—a grassroots organization committed to creating unique spaces for unlikely partners to engage in hard, heartfelt conversations on difficult subjects—please visit www .fearlessdialogues.com.

FEARLESS DIALOGUES™

A New Movement for Justice

GREGORY C. ELLISON II

WJK WESTMINSTER
JOHN KNOX PRESS
LOUISVILLE · KENTUCKY

© 2017 Gregory C. Ellison II
Foreword © 2017 Westminster John Knox Press

First edition
Published by Westminster John Knox Press
Louisville, Kentucky

17 18 19 20 21 22 23 24 25 26—10 9 8 7 6 5 4 3 2 1

Scripture taken from the Holy Bible, New International Reader's Version®.Copyright © 1996,
1998 Biblica. All rights reserved throughout the world. Used by permission of Biblica. Scripture
quotations marked NLT are taken from the Holy Bible, New Living Translation, copyright
1996, 2004. Used by permission of Tyndale House Publishers, Inc., Wheaton, Illinois 60189.
All rights reserved.

Excerpt from Lucille Clifton, "seeker of visions" from *The Book of Light*. Copyright © 1993 by Lucille
Clifton. Reprinted with the permission of The Permissions Company, Inc. on behalf of Copper Canyon
Press, www.coppercanyonpress.org. Excerpt from "The Third Sermon on the Warpland," in
The Essential Gwendolyn Brooks, ed. Elizabeth Alexander (New York: Library of America, 2005)
is reprinted by consent of Brooks Permissions.

*Illustration in chapter 5 is by Reynolds / fotolia by Adobe and is used by permission. Photo in chapter 6 is by
Wiley Price/St. Louis American and is used by permission.*

Book design by Drew Stevens
Cover design by Allison Taylor

Library of Congress Cataloging-in-Publication Data
Names: Ellison, Gregory C., II, author.
Title: Fearless dialogues : a new movement for justice / Gregory C. Ellison
    II.
Description: First edition. | Louisville, KY : Westminster John Knox Press,
    2017. | Includes index. |
Identifiers: LCCN 2017023311 (print) | LCCN 2017046460 (ebook) | ISBN
    9781611648348 (ebk.) | ISBN 9780664260651 (pbk. : alk. paper)
Subjects: LCSH: African American youth--Social conditions. | African
    Americans--Social conditions. | Social change--United States.
Classification: LCC E185.86 (ebook) | LCC E185.86 .E4373 2017 (print) | DDC
    305.235089/96--dc23
LC record available at https://lccn.loc.gov/2017023311

♾ The paper used in this publication meets the minimum requirements
of the American National Standard for Information Sciences—Permanence of Paper
for Printed Library Materials, ANSI Z39.48-1992.

Contents

Foreword

In the summer of 2013, Greg Ellison, professor at Candler School of Theology at Emory University in Atlanta, Georgia, reached out to me for a conversation. I'm forever grateful that he did.

That November, Greg visited me at home in Madison, Wisconsin. For two days, Greg and I, joined at times by my wife, Sharon, sat on our back porch talking, laughing, and breaking bread together. We did what people do when they meet on the porch, not in the office: we told stories of our lives and opened our hearts to each other. In the process, two people in their seventies found a dear friend in this remarkable man who's half our age.

At one point Greg read us a piece he had written for the book you now hold in your hands. Sharon and I were mesmerized by the story of an experience Greg once had on another porch—his grandmother's front porch in Arkansas, at night, where he sat as she helped him at age six overcome his fear of the dark.

When Greg finished reading, my wife and I sat in silence for a moment, looking at him through teary eyes. "Greg," I said, "you've hit bedrock."

Greg asked what I meant. "You're writing from the deepest place in you, the only place worth writing from, a place from which flows a universal language. Forget all that marketing stuff. Don't write *to* a 'target audience.' Write *from* the deepest place in yourself, and your writing will connect with the deepest place in a wider range of people than you can imagine." That is exactly what Greg has done in this book.

Flash forward to May 3, 2017. Sharon and I were in a Minneapolis hotel ballroom with 650 people who work in ministry and theological education. We were there to participate in a session called "Fearless Dialogues," led by Greg Ellison.

I imagine the audience was expecting a lecture by this young but already distinguished African American scholar, teacher, and activist, who holds a PhD from Princeton Theological Seminary. But that's not what they got, praise be!

Instead, they got a mind-body-spirit engagement, a live encounter, with a remarkable teacher, with each other, and with a world of great need. It's a world in which we have forgotten that what makes a society great is not how well the strongest can do, but how well we support the poor and the marginalized, the rejected and the unseen.

Greg's session was scheduled to begin at nine o'clock; but when that hour came, and even fifteen minutes later, he was not up front making opening remarks. Instead, he was moving among the crowd, coming up close to people, looking them in the eye, and saying, loudly and with conviction, "It is good to finally see you!" As the time ticked by, 650 folks began to realize that they were in for something different!

What followed was the process described in this remarkable book. It's a process that left me and many others in that Minneapolis ballroom stunned and deeply moved, as Greg reminded us—and gave us ways to remind each other—of the humanity and divinity of every human being, the qualities that alone can save us and our shared world.

When the session was over, I heard others say what I was feeling: "I'm so glad I was here." "I've never experienced anything like this." "I feel like some sort of wall has come down inside of me."

Fearless Dialogues—like the organization that bears its name—is rich with penetrating insights and practical approaches to some of America's deepest and most intractable social needs. Equally important, it is grounded in stories drawn from Greg's life that reveal the deep, broad root system of his remarkable brand of scholarship, teaching, and activism.

Greg's first book bears the revealing title *Cut Dead But Still Alive: Caring for African American Young Men* (2013). The title comes from William James, who explains it this way in one of his masterworks, *The Principles of Psychology* (1890):

> If no one turned around when we entered, answered when we spoke, or minded what we did, but if every person we met "cut us dead," and acted as if we were non-existent things, a kind of rage and impotent despair would before long well up in us, from which the cruelest bodily torture would be a relief.

That, of course, is the true meaning of Greg's signature greeting to participants in the "Fearless Dialogue" program: "It is good to finally see you!" As Greg has said,

It is my hope that this book will help us to see all people in a more human and even a more divine way: That we are all worthy of respect. That we are all worthy of an opportunity to succeed.

As a white, straight, privileged male, I have another hope for myself and all who read this powerful book. Let us first look at *ourselves* through the lenses Greg Ellison offers us in this book. Let us come to terms with our own failure to see, truly see, certain individuals because they are not of "our tribe," or because they frighten us, or because they don't fit our notions of beauty or propriety. Only then can we truly begin the see "the other." To quote Greg again,

> Once you begin to see a person as one who is made in the image of God, once you begin to see a homeless person as someone's uncle or brother or aunt or sister or mother, you can't just step over them like a piece of trash, because you have seen them fully. . . . Once you see, you cannot not see.

Read this book! It will change you, as it has changed me, if you can say and truly mean, "It is good to finally see you!" Then you will be able to help change whatever part of the world is within your reach.

In closing, I want to return to our back porch in Madison, Wisconsin. During our November 2013 conversation, Greg asked me to tell him about my journey as a writer. Along the way, I told a story about my friendship with the late Henri Nouwen, a story that Greg found striking.

I met Henri when I was about Greg's age now, and had just begun to work on my first book. Henri, only seven years my senior, was already a well-known and very popular writer, while I—unlike Greg—was largely unknown. For two academic years, Henri and I spent a day together every other week. From time to time, I talked about the book I was working on.

One day Henri said, "Let me see what you've got." After reading a few chapters, Henri asked if it would be OK with me if he wrote a foreword to the book. I remember saying, "Um, Henri, OK is *way* too mild a word. *Wahoo!* or *Whoopee!* would be closer to the mark!"

Today, nine books later, it's clear that Henri's foreword to *The Promise of Paradox* helped put my work on the map and extend my reach as a writer. So for years I've wanted to "pay forward" Henri's gift to me by supporting younger writers on their way.

There's no one whom I'd sooner support than Greg Ellison. In his work and in his person, he's offering the world gifts that we sorely need.

Fearless Dialogues is one of those gifts. Take it, open it, learn from it, and act—for the sake of a better world.

Parker J. Palmer

Acknowledgments

A Letter to My Son on the One Hundred Fifty-Fourth Anniversary of the Emancipation

01 January 2017
Atlanta, Georgia

Dear Gregory:

In the quiet sanctity of the early morn, I close my eyes and see the dawning smile of innocence break across the horizon of your sister's face. Though you are only two years her senior, and not even in your tenth year, you meet the day with a furrowed brow and with eyes clouded by hard questions: "In this new administration, will our Muslim cousins have to leave the United States? If global warming continues, what kind of world will my grandkids live in? Another Black boy, really? Why did they kill him? Am I safe?" The intensity of your questions gives me pause and lights my fire. But you are not the only one concerned with life's hard questions. Since 2013, you have watched my colleagues and me create spaces for communities to engage in heartfelt conversations on taboo subjects. These communities also seek answers. Yet, we encourage them to not rush toward solutions at the expense of neglecting the unacknowledged all around them. Your questions and theirs have driven me to write.

This book is our story. It is our song. In these pages, you will encounter how unlikely partners have worked to build community in the face of daunting fear. The life lessons of these master practitioners are placed alongside the works of theorists renowned the world over. But, as I have taught you, Son, teachers come in all shapes and forms. Give thanks with me for the educators who have published many books and shared their works in university lecture halls and show gratitude to gurus like your great-grandmothers who transformed rickety porches and kitchen tables into classrooms that enlivened prophetic imagination. In this book, I share only a thimble-full of lessons learned from this sundry of sages, but I pray that in the melodic recounting of their stories my homage to their truths will reverberate in your soul.

As an aspiring musician, you understand that while most composers fall within a tradition, some seek a unique sound. This publication is my first attempt to write from a deeper register and attune my writer's voice to a sound authentic to me. From day one, Bob Ratcliff and his colleagues at Westminster John Knox Press have pushed me to uncover the genuine sound of my authorial voice. Likewise, Don Richter of the Louisville Institute and my family at the Forum for Theological Exploration have beckoned me to write from my diaphragm. Classes of students and gatherings of faculty at Emory University's Candler School of Theology, Sewanee's School of Theology, Eden Theological Seminary, Princeton Theological Seminary, and Yale Divinity School afforded me opportunities to test my vocal cords as a writer. They also kindly informed me when my notes were off-key. More than an audition, this book is concerto number one.

You know well that this is not a solo act. At each step along the way, I have been accompanied by artists, healers, educators, activists, connectors, and neighbors. Each, in their own way, has contributed to the scoring of this book and to the evolution of Fearless Dialogues. I tip my hat to Andrea Bryant, Eunhil David Cho, Leah Clements, Michelly Furtado, Nelson Furtado, Alisha "Radio" Gordon, Nicole Hepp, Okorie Johnson, Andre Ledgister, Georgette "JoJo" Ledgister, Jill Morehouse Lum, Staci Lynch, John Majors, Megan McCamey, Lynn Miller, Iyabo Onipede, Bridget Piggue, Julian Reid, Quentin Samuel, Rodney Shamery, Sonny Smith, Tavares Stephens, Calvin Taylor, Zachary Thompson, and Sam White. So, too must I acknowledge each of the community partners from Leadership Atlanta, the Lovett Schools, and the churches, communities, and corporations that have afforded us space to craft a new song.

Someday you and your sister will read these pages and gain a glimpse of my inner world. My explorations of this inner terrain are as instructive as any book read or conversation held. Please know that in sharing these insights, I have not only weighed the personal and professional risks of vulnerability but also sought wise counsel at every turn from my Yodas: Emanuel Cleaver II, Mari Evans, James "Brother Rabbi" Kynes, Parker J. Palmer, Sharon Palmer, Helen Pearson Smith, Luther Smith Jr., Barbara Brown Taylor, and Ed Taylor. You should also know a few others who have trekked with me as I explored the interior and walked through the door no person could shut: James Brown, Dwight Davis, Kenya Davis, Dukens Falaise, C. Douglas Hollis Jr., Michelle

Ledder, Stephen Lewis, Shimba Mulunda, Cezanne Pace, Toby Sanders, Simon, Brandon Williams, Matthew Wesley Williams, and Floyd Wood II. The more you learn about this cadre of folk, the more you will know about me. For each of these fellow sojourners, I give thanks.

Finally, I could not walk this road without the presence and prayerful support of the folk in our bloodline. For their companionship and love, I express heartfelt thanks to the Day, Dixon, Ellison, Greenaway, Powell, Rollins, and Watts families. You know that Greg Sr., Jeannette, and Darren propped me up when my sides were leaning. Your brother, Elisha, sat with me on the late nights when the words would not come. Your beloved sister, Anaya, reminded me to hope on the eves when terrors showed up unaware. Since our first date in 2001, your mother, Antoinette, has pushed me to realize my fullest potential and to settle for nothing less than excellence. For each and every person, named and unnamed, who has accompanied me on this journey, I give thanks.

Last, you, my beloved namesake, are the window to my soul. May the peace of the eternal God guide your every step.

Your father,

Greg

1

Fear+Less Dialogues Introduced

No dogs nip at my heels as I outstretch the three-feet measuring tape overhead, but I feel the ancestral presence of freedom fighters hoisting picket signs. With fists clenched on each side of the measuring tape, I sense a kinship with young activists who throw up their arms in protest and bow their knee to die-in. Unchoked by tear gas, my legs stand firm. But my unclouded eyes still water as I recall the faces of a hundred hues.

For a solitary moment, I gaze silently into the eyes of remembered faces standing before me. They too hold three-feet measuring tapes above their heads. Through my watery eyes, I see them clearly. There is the former gang leader in New Orleans with the garish knife wound chiseled around his neck from ear to ear. To his left, the Spanish-speaking New York pastor and the wheelchaired activist from Georgia. My eyes continue to rove the room and I peep the quizzical grin of the aging white male business tycoon. Next to him, I behold the prophetic vision of the brown-faced girl from Ferguson, who saw a flash of heaven in her community where others saw only hell. I look around the room and recall the faces of thousands of unlikely partners drawn together by Fearless Dialogues for hard heartfelt conversations. . . . Then I see Monique Rivarde.

Twelve months before Fearless Dialogues entered public discourse, I met Monique in a crowded courtroom. A cloud cover of rage hovered over the sentencing, and teardrops showered down this mother's cheeks. Nevertheless, undeterred by fear, Monique looked squarely into the eyes of the murderers of her eighteen-year-old son and challenged them to commit to become better men. Not once did Monique raise her voice, but when she spoke, people leaned in closer to hear. Months later in a Fearless Dialogues community conversation about police brutality, Monique sat amid a cloud of witnesses numbering nearly two hundred and offered another challenge: See and hear the pains of the unacknowledged all around us. Her words reverberated through every soul in the room. Again, she spoke barely above a thunderous whisper.

Rivarde represents a form of resistance that is quiet and forceful. According to Kevin Quashie, "resistance" that is solely described as a deafening outcry "is too clunky, vague and imprecise to be a catch-all for a whole range of human behaviors and ambitions."[1] When quiet resistance is overlooked in history, it is possible to uplift the strides of televised protests and stamp out the acts of day-to-day resistance of the millions, like Monique, who will never make the headlines. Fearless Dialogues equips communities to see the invisible, to hear the muted, and to create change through quiet resistance and fearless speech.

THE BIRTH OF FEARLESS DIALOGUES

Seeking Truth through Troth

It was a sweltering afternoon in May 2013, yet colleague after colleague filed into the conference room. The summer seminar doubled as a think tank, and all in attendance were primed for conversation and eager to bring to life theories from my first book, *Cut Dead but Still Alive: Caring for African American Young Men*. Twelve in total, we encircled the conference table. Before speaking I scanned the room and took notice of these unlikely partners. Around the table were a power-plant engineer, a marketing executive, a graphic designer, a community organizer, a drug dealer turned artist, an IT specialist, a freelance journalist, a professional singer, a pastor, a fashion designer, and a corporate attorney. Once the room settled, I quietly searched the eyes of every individual in the circle. Behind every cornea, I saw a story. Beyond every iris, there lay a gift. In the silence that followed, I could sense the ancestors and archangels blessing the work before us and the unborn unbridling our tongues. Breaking through with quiet resistance, I uttered seven simple words of invocation, "It is good to finally see you."

For the next hour, full-hearted introductions flowed freely in the space; it was evident that this gathering of gifted persons possessed great potential for catalyzing change. Yet between introductions, a discomforting silence lingered near. A closer look revealed that subtle smiles and uneasy laughter masked a nervous energy. Person after person recounted grim tales of similar gatherings of impassioned leaders. Each of these narratives echoed a tragic cycle:

— Impassioned leaders gather.
— The perils of paternalism, territorialism, and fear stifle conversation.
— With no framework for dialogue, the leaders retreat to familiar theories, practices, and dogmas.
— Creativity, collaboration, and change dissipate.
— Frustrated leaders depart.
— Seeking to chart a course that would avoid dialogical derailment, we declared a troth.

Centuries ago, individuals and communities inscribed sacred bonds with each other by declaring a troth. The Old English word "troth" is an ancient vow where persons or communities entered a covenant to engage in a mutually accountable and transforming relationship. These solemn promises forged relationships of trust and faith in the face of unknowable risks.[2] Our troth was simple. We covenanted to train our eyes to see individuals and communities hidden in plain view. We vowed to attune our ears to hear the muted who scream from the shadows. During our training and attunement, we pledged to remain in community and to address any rising discord in our group with courage and humility. This troth would illumine our way and guide our interactions.

For weeks we read, ate, and shared together. We were far from an ordinary class; the city was our laboratory. So together we walked urban streets, learning from community organizers and local pastors, swapping stories with griot-like grandmothers and down-to-earth drug dealers. In time, we recognized small yet noticeable shifts in the world around us. We were seeing differently. We were hearing differently. We were changing internally.

But just as our vision was clarifying, blind rage circulated on social media. Though we were hearing more deeply, we could not ignore the fever pitch of discord scouring national news:

George Zimmerman Found Not Guilty and Goes Free[3]

Twitter Erupts After Ex-Neighborhood Watchman Walks on . . .
Murder Charge[4]

Ivy League Professor Calls "God a Racist" after Zimmerman
Verdict

Verdict Doesn't End Debate in Trayvon Martin Death

'No Justice': Thousands March for Trayvon Martin[5]

After Zimmerman Verdict, Trayvon Martin Isn't Only Victim[6]

President Obama: Trayvon Martin Could Have Been Me[7]

White Churches Uncommonly Quiet after Zimmerman Verdict[8]

In the days following the July 13, 2013, verdict that found George
Zimmerman not guilty for the murder of Trayvon Martin, constructive
conversations seized. At dinner tables and lunch counters, dialogues
were wedged between screams for justice and silent sorrow. Thousands
jammed onto city streets and civic squares in protest, while even more
sat at home in moral conflict, questioning their complicity or justify-
ing their silence in fear of being labeled a bigot. A space was needed
for hard heartfelt conversations that could transform a powder keg of
emotion into a creative medium for change.

The time had come for Fearless Dialogues to move from theory to
practice. So the twelve who gathered around that conference table in
May sent out a call to action on social media, public radio, and print
media: "We will have a community conversation about the Zimmerman verdict on July 20, 2013. All are welcome!"

Heaven on Earth: A Movement Unfolds

Rain pelted the summer-scorched concrete and steam rose like a numi-
nous fog. Despite the traffic jams that gripped Atlanta, three hundred
people bypassed bottlenecks and navigated side streets to find their
way to Emory University. Each was unsatisfied with age-old options
of writing their congressperson or toting placards on the capitol steps.
Some needed a place to be seen and chose to no longer scream from
the shadows. Others sought a space to hear the opinions of real people,
not just thoughts of political pundits. Sifting through the fog, they
searched for change . . . and we welcomed them with Radical Hospitality in the parking lot. Each person received the same introduction:

"It is good to finally see you. Welcome to Fearless Dialogues. Are you ready for change?"

As they entered the building, live music colored the air. Standing at a registration table adjacent to the door, a Fearless Dialogues team member greeted each person again with the same three prompts: "It is good to finally see you. Welcome to Fearless Dialogues. Are you ready for change?"

At this table, the dialogue continued as the community leaders gathering for conversation selected name tags that uniquely described the gifts of their soul. A judge chose a name tag that read "healer." Emory's assistant provost picked a name tag reading "artist." A single mother placed an "educator" name tag on her dress, while a factory worker selected a name tag labeled "neighbor."[9] Once self-identified by their gifts, community leaders were invited upstairs by another Fearless Dialogues team member, who offered our signature salutation once more: "It is good to finally see you. Welcome to Fearless Dialogues. Are you ready for change?"

Overwrought by seven days of sensationalized media slander, schism, and debate over Zimmerman's not-guilty verdict, these three hundred people proudly, even if tentatively, wore their soul-gifts on display. Many came seeking to understand and to be understood. Some sought a shoulder to cry on, while others yearned for a venue to vent. Jam-packed in the room, we anticipated hard conversation, but we could not pinpoint exactly what might happen that evening. After preliminary introductions and an explanation of the Fearless Dialogues philosophy, groups were divided based on the name tags chosen during registration. Not only did neighbors sit around tables with artists, healers, and educators. These groups also brought foundation executives, small-nonprofit leaders, factory workers, students, and drug dealers face-to-face.

Before the community conversation began, we introduced the Fearless Dialogues "animators" in the room. Unlike workshop facilitators, who call out participants raising their hands or waiting their turn to speak, Fearless Dialogues animators are uniquely trained to bring conversations to life. These animators give inspiration, encouragement, and renewed vigor to unlikely partners in dialogue.

After the animators laid out the ground rules for dialogue, they guided these small groups into conversation. On that first day, we had not yet developed our signature-theory based experiments, but the twelve of us who sat around that conference table and walked the city streets together noticed an uptick of hope as the exchanges between the three hundred deepened. Lifted by the energy of connecting with unlikely partners in hard heartfelt conversation, the three hundred ended their time together by hoisting three-feet measuring tapes in the air and accepting a simple challenge.

Nearly an hour after taking the three-feet challenge, the band had played their last note, but the steady hum of conversation continued. Dozens of unlikely partners clung to the moment and remained deeply engaged in dialogue. We underestimated the impact of Radical Hospitality. We underappreciated the value of crafting space for unlikely partners to see the invisible and hear the muted. Then I had an unforgettable encounter as I exited the building.

Nearly out the door, one young man who sold drugs pulled me to the side and looked deeply into my eyes. Little did I know that his words would catalyze our movement. The words fell from his lips with a thick southern twang: "This felt like heaven. I haven't been in many places where I can share my story and how I feel without being judged."

Two days later, the twelve regathered around the conference table. Over a meal we recounted the moments on that Saturday afternoon when the dean saw the gifts in the drug dealer, the factory worker heard the vulnerabilities of the foundation executive, and the graduate student and the grieving mother envisioned communal change. On that rainy afternoon, we received a glimpse of heaven on earth. On July 20, 2013, human action collided with divine intervention, and Fearless Dialogues was born.

FEAR+LESS DIALOGUES

Fearless Dialogues is a grassroots nonprofit initiative committed to creating unique spaces for unlikely partners to engage in hard heartfelt conversations that see gifts in others, hear value in stories, and work for change and positive transformation in self and other. Thinking critically about the words "fear" and "less" individually, and then as a compound word, is central to the work of Fearless Dialogues. I invite you to consider these three words now.

Fear, noun \fi(ə)r\
    an unpleasant emotion caused by the belief that someone or something is dangerous, likely to cause pain, or a threat.

Like thin air leaking out of an airtight room, fear stifles, closes in, and isolates. Hounding us by day and harrowing by night, fear "lurks ready to spring into action as soon as one is alone, or as soon as the lights go out, or as soon as one's social defenses are temporarily removed."[10] This pervasive fear expects conflict and roots itself in the "heart of relationships between the weak and the strong, between the controllers of the environment and those who are controlled by it."[11] Often fear appears one-sided, as the weak are seemingly intimidated by the strong. However, an undiscussed and undisclosed fear also lingers in the hearts of many strong persons in power. They fear the possibility of being forcefully knocked from their pedestal. One debilitating result of fear is the inability to see beyond the facade of power or the visage of weakness and to glimpse the power that lies within. For meaningful connections to be forged, individuals and communities must face fear head on.

Less, det. & pronoun \les\
　　a smaller amount of, not as much

An antidote to fear, "lessness" is a posture of humility, perceptiveness, and intention not to lord power over others. This posture resists the temptations of possessing all the answers, and yields to the mysterious journey of raising questions. Lessness is not a diminishment of control. To the contrary, this posture requires attunement and discipline to listen first and not battle for the last word, to see a gift where others see only problems. In a dialogical landscape where news pundits shout down adversaries in their fear of losing ground or being wrong, Fearless Dialogues models another way to engage. Less is more.

Fear -less, adj \fi(ə)r\ + \les\
　　~~lacking fear~~

I have intentionally struck through the most common definition of "fearless" because this definitions rings untrue for the work of Fearless Dialogues. In its most common usage, "fearless" is the composition of a root and a suffix ("fear" and "-less"). Here, the suffix "less" means "without." This construction connotes that hard heartfelt conversations can exist without the presence of fear. However, seldom is it the case that unlikely partners, whether self-identified by their soul-gifts or not, can engage in hard heartfelt conversation with absolutely no fear.

Fear + less, adj \fi(ə)r\ + \les\
　　compound word addressing the reality of fear and the possibility of "less-ness" to free unlikely partners to have hard heartfelt conversations.

A preferred structure for the work of convening unlikely partners is to define the word "fearless" by viewing the term as a compound word ("fear" + "less"). With a compound structure in mind, "less" means "to a smaller extent," suggesting that when fears are named, they have less of a stranglehold on hard conversations. Further, "less" evokes images of a disciplined posture of lessness between conversation partners. Thus, as a compound word, "fear+less" dialogues offers greater possibilities for unlikely partners to engage challenging subjects together.

UNLIKELY PARTNERS TOO NUMEROUS TO COUNT

Fearless Dialogues is unique in scope because of its value of bringing unlikely partners into common spaces for dialogue. In the first Fearless Dialogues community conversation, faculty, students, staff, and administrators from Emory University found common ground with judges, foundation executives, factory workers, elected officials, drug dealers, and physicians. Since that summer afternoon in 2013, Fearless Dialogues has gathered more than 15,000 unlikely partners for community conversations in college classrooms, corporate boardrooms, church sanctuaries, and community centers. Whether working with incarcerated youth, community organizers, education professionals, or trustee boards, Fearless Dialogues emphasizes that even those who share common space with us daily may still occupy the role of Familiar Strangers. Therefore, we create conditions for unlikely partners like the judge and the felon, the rich and the poor, the old and the young to see and hear each other in new and enriching ways.

This book outlines the methodology of Fearless Dialogues by simulating a community conversation between unlikely partners. Within these pages you will notice theoretical voices from pastoral theology, Quaker philosophy, African American history, and twentieth-century mysticism, alongside the ancestral wisdom from the Black literary tradition. You will overhear formative moments from my youth, behold the timeless wisdom of my grandparents, and listen to transformative encounters from Fearless Dialogues gatherings. Just as hard heartfelt conversations between corporate executives and artists or gang members and stay-at-home moms are critical for the "work" of Fearless Dialogues, so also is the cacophony of dialogue partners within these pages vital to our learning. For the Fearless Dialogues method to remain authentic, its methodology must not justify the ends but rather practice them.

As author, I accept the honor of "animating" the dialogue in this book. During Fearless Dialogues conversations, animators utilize an unconventional combination of interactive exercises, small- and large-group reflection, and high-impact theory-based lectures, all wrapped in the posture of "lessness" and in the arms of Radical Hospitality. In this role, I am privileged to guide you through theory and practices that have made the work of Fearless Dialogues meaningful for countless unlikely partners.

My freewheeling style of writing—from poetry and prose to cultural criticism and historical snapshots—mirrors my approach to teaching and counseling, which maintains that animators must capture the audience's imagination in seconds, lest these animators find themselves tuned out and invisible. The poetry, prose, and creative writing are intended to stimulate the imagination of the artists. Attention to the mystical tradition and practices to foster individual and collective wholeness may resonate with the healers. The close examination of theoretical sources and attention to multisensory learning styles may refresh the minds and hearts of educators. The neighbors are invited to feel connection in the varied experiments formed in the laboratory of discovery. Activists might use this text as a barometer to measure their sensitivity to seeing, hearing, and standing alongside those who remain unacknowledged and marginalized. Finally, the connectors may engage in a meta-analysis of how Fearless Dialogues animators bring conversations to life while carefully balancing strong personalities and unstable power dynamics.

Finally, since this work is not a Fearless Monologue, you will be invited into the conversation as well. Throughout the book, as I move between theory, practice, and narrative, I pose italicized questions directly to you, Beloved Reader. As these questions bear deep philosophical and vocational weight, you may choose to respond with your voice by scribbling thoughts and feelings directly into the margin or in a nearby journal. While this is not a workbook, the pages following are written to evoke conversation with others and provoke a deep and interrogating conversation with self. Since some of the moments of this book are especially tense, be aware of times when I invite you to breathe, stretch, or observe silence. Please accept my invitation to you, Beloved Reader, to join Fearless Dialogues as our latest unlikely partner. "It is good to finally see you. Welcome to Fearless Dialogues. Are you ready for change?"

THE JOURNEY AHEAD

In Fearless Dialogues' work with thousands of unlikely partners and dozens of communities around the globe, my colleagues and I have noticed five primary fears that stifle conversation: the fear of the unknown, the fear of strangers, the fear of plopping, the fear of appearing ignorant, and the fear of oppressive systems. Each of the five remaining chapters examines how Fearless Dialogues utilizes theories and practices to overcome these fears that impede meaningful exchange.

Creating unique spaces for hard heartfelt conversation is the niche of Fearless Dialogues and our response to the perilous fear of the unknown. In a conversation with country dark, chapter 2 moves us into the luminous darkness. Surrounded by the magic of country dark, I share with you how Fearless Dialogues creates spaces that embrace failure, stimulate the senses, and identify pockets of freedom. I am certain that my Grandma's wisdom and Barbara Brown Taylor's sacramental vision will make altars of the spaces in which you move.

At my maternal grandmother's welcome table, we learned to lessen our fears of strangers. Chapter 3 introduces Fearless Dialogues' unique approaches to Radical Hospitality. Guided by soul-stirring narratives and conversations with diverse theorists like mystic and educator Parker J. Palmer, pastoral theologian Robert C. Dykstra, social psychologist Stanley Milgram, and my gun-toting Granma, you will feast at the welcome table with Public Strangers, Familiar Strangers, Intimate Strangers, and the Stranger Within.

Have you ever shared your truth in a classroom, a boardroom, or your family dinner table, only to have your cherished words crash to the floor with no response? Master educator Jane Vella calls this painful experience of not being valued as a speaker "plopping." In chapter 4, to examine the fear of plopping, I recount my own educational journey from an inner-city high school in Atlanta to the hallowed halls of Princeton's Ivy Green. Lessons from these institutions of higher learning and theories from psychologist William James and social psychologist Kipling Williams inform how Fearless Dialogues helps unlikely partners to see the unacknowledged all around us.

"I am unfit. I feel unequipped. I feel unprepared." These three insecurities mask a fear of appearing ignorant. In chapter 5, I share Fearless
Dialogues' threefold approach to peeling away these masking insecurities. As you learn to increase proximity, listen empathically, and inquire
humbly, I introduce you to the works of sociologist James A. Vela-
McConnell, pastoral theologian Karen Scheib, and the Carmelite monk
William McNamara. Perhaps more compelling is my invitation for you
to descend with me into the belly of the beast, where we will take A
Long Loving Look at the Real and face life's Five Hardest Questions.

"I am not an activist because I don't . . ." Far too many change
agents are immobilized by oppressive systems that predetermine the
acceptable parameters of activism. To face the fear of oppressive systems and move beyond vocations of negation, chapter 6 asks the bone-
chilling question "What must I do to die a good death?" Guided by the
adolescent lives of Martin Luther, Howard Thurman, Jesus Christ, and
my childhood hero, together we will be galvanized to change the three
feet around us.

THREE FEET, THREE WORDS, THREE PILLARS

Whether standing in an auditorium in Nassau, a classroom in Sao
Paulo, a concert hall in Atlanta, or a church in Memphis, I issue the
same challenge to the remembered faces holding a three-feet measuring
tape overhead. As we look eye to eye, I share the Fearless Dialogues ral-
lying cry, a life-changing story from my childhood:

> This may come as no surprise to you, but I was a strange child who
> asked big questions. After all, I was reared in the home of activ-
> ists, and I walked the hills of Atlanta in the shadows of the Mar-
> tin Luther King Jr. Center. In all her wisdom, my Aunt Dotty was
> unalarmed when I, at eight years old, asked how I could change the
> world. Honoring my boyish justice impulse, she responded, "Baby,
> I don't know how to change the world, but I can change the three
> feet around me."

Over three decades since that porchside chat with Aunt Dotty,
the Fearless Dialogues team has challenged more than 15,000 people
worldwide to see the lives and hear the stories of three people who cross
within their three feet. The three-feet challenge anchors this new movement for justice.

It may sound unconventional to hear that Fearless Dialogues measures both local and global change in thirty-six-inch increments. Built on the cornerstone of my personal mantra, "Once you see, you cannot not see," at base level Fearless Dialogues encourages community leaders to become fully aware of the people and resources existent within their three-feet orbit. Equipped with heightened awareness of the potential gifts and valued assets within arm's reach, community leaders come to experience an altered vision that changes how they move in the world. For instance, once you truly come to see a maître d', a drug dealer, a homeless person, or a traumatized teenager as someone made in the image of God, with a potential and perhaps undiscovered gift that can change the course of a community, you can no longer disregard that human being. You can no longer overlook them, bypass them, or step over them, because you have seen them cross within your three feet . . . and once you see, you cannot not see.

The Fearless Dialogues three-feet challenge stands firmly on three feet, or shall I say, three pillars: See. Hear. Change. In my years of research on marginalization, muteness, and invisibility, I have come to believe that purposeful engagement and sustainable change are not possible while community partners remain unseen and unheard.[12] For this reason, Fearless Dialogues places primacy on seeing and hearing as gateways to change. More specifically, we believe that when unlikely partners come to see individuals around them as innately gifted human beings, then they can hear the stories of people from seemingly different backgrounds as valuable. With the capacity to see gifts and hear wisdom within unfamiliar stories, the pump is primed for unlikely partners to pursue change. These three pillars—See, Hear, Change— are indelibly infused into the theory and practice of Fearless Dialogues.

As is illustrated throughout this book, to *see* is much more than to behold with the eye, because "vision is one of the laziest senses."[13] The full sensory nature of seeing became clear to me years ago when I had the pleasure of visiting the New York art studio of the internationally renowned Japanese American artist Makoto "Mako" Fujimura. Upon my entering the lofted space, an aromatic admixture of metal dust, saturated paper, and acrylic paints traveled through my nostrils and settled in my throat. The smell and taste of the space immediately transformed my preconceived notion of an art studio into an alchemist lab. As I touched the fine-ground gold dust that layers Mako's paintings, I came to see his works with greater texture and meaning. Akin to Fujimura's alchemist-like art studio, Fearless Dialogues creates unique spaces that heighten sensory awareness. Utilizing visual art, music, and interactive exercises, this hypersensory environment, known as the Laboratory of Discovery, aids community partners in "seeing" the gifts in themselves and in those around them.

The art of *hearing* is also multitextured. One must train the ear, intensify the imagination, and expand levels of empathy to hear value in the stories of others who are seemingly different. Laden in the theory and practice of Fearless Dialogues one finds the benefits of carefully listening both to piercing rage and quiet courage. Consistent with the musical symbolism throughout this book, my piano teacher, Simon, once told me, "When life is hard, music makes it easier to breathe." Likewise, in the heat of hard heartfelt conversations, an ear attuned to hope can provide a pocket of air for unlikely partners suffocated by problems that seem asphyxiating.

The great cultural anthropologist Margaret Mead once said, "Never doubt that a small group of committed citizens can change the world. Indeed, it is the only thing that ever has." Embracing Mead's aspiration, Fearless Dialogues maintains that global *change* embraces the paradoxical tensions of narrative, space, and time. As is reiterated throughout this book, small, seemingly insignificant practices can precipitate lasting change. When ordinary individuals fearlessly commit to changing the three feet around them, the tectonic plates of a community shift. Finally, Fearless Dialogues creates crucible moments for time-bending transformation that emerge when human interaction collides with divine intervention. In these rare moments, the past is reframed, future possibilities appear attainable, the present is energized with hope, and the kingdom of God descends to earth. For Fearless Dialogues, change is both local and global; it transforms individuals and multiple generations; it collapses time to clarify vision; and it energizes the heads and hearts of unlikely partners.

THE QUIET COURAGE TO SPEAK AND TO BE

In a national climate where political pundits spar on television, and social media debates end in stalemate, there are few models that demonstrate conversation across lines of difference. Yet families, churches, schools, and corporations desire pathways to engage in meaningful conversations and face difficult subjects. Perhaps this is why you have chosen this book. In the pages that follow, I will share with you how

Fearless Dialogues creates unique spaces for unlikely partners to over-come fears and engage in hard heartfelt conversation. Together, we will embark on a journey of self-examination and explore how social change is spurred by deep engagement with the variety of people who cross within our three feet. As you muster the quiet courage to speak and to be, I extend this invitation to you, Beloved Reader: Welcome to Fear-less Dialogues! It is good to finally see you. Are you ready for change? Let's get to work!

2

Conversations with Country Dark

Beyond the Fear of the Unknown

My citified eyes were unprepared for country dark. Under the expanse of an unlit sky, my six-year-old hand was undetectable just inches from my face. Disembodied in this darkness, a shrieking chill shivered across my skin. For the first two evenings this unknown fear pulsed through my veins and stole my shut-eye. So as the sun lay down on day three, she welcomed me to a most unlikely classroom and altered my vision for life.

Three days before my late-night lesson, Grandma and I boarded a bus in Kansas City with two bags of clothes, a box of chicken, and a tin of oatmeal cookies, en route to her hometown in Arkansas. As the bus rolled into town, I immediately noticed that there were no streetlights to illumine the gravel paths in Grandma's old stomping ground. Just steps off the bus, I unsuccessfully sought my hand. It was "blacker than a hundred midnights down in a cypress swamp."[1]

After two eves of night terrors, Grandma took me out on the porch of her sister's shotgun house and opened her lecture with these timeless words: "Country dark is God's gift to your senses." When the sun nestled down for an evening rest, she pulled out an old ice-cream maker and told me to turn the crank. Ice crunched, rock salt crackled, and the dairy tin spun round and round. As I focused on the spinning tin, hypnotically I entered a time machine of sorts. The hour hand froze. The second hand slowed. The ominous night became luminous. Then her lecture unfolded something like this . . .

15

There are some things you can only experience in the denseness of the dark. "What do you feel?" A flutter of lightning bugs' wings suddenly fanned my face as they twinkled and twirled before me. "That's God bringing the stars of the heavens down to earth."

"Listen closely. What do you hear?" It was an outdoor symphony. Like frictionless bows gliding across four-stringed violins, a chorus of cricket legs scratched out a most natural tune.

"Stick out your tongue. Your taste buds can see too." That night she taught me how to taste the sweet kiss of coming rain.

Time unfroze. What seemed to be milliseconds were actually hours. On that porch, my unknown fears melted away and I slept like a newborn. Three decades later, a pitch-black night still smells like homespun ice cream.

Today, in the sweet bliss of distant memory, hard questions sour my nostalgia: Were my childhood fears of darkness baseless? Was the fright lurking behind my undetectable six-year-old hand learned or innate? Have the unknown fears of yesteryear cast shadows on my adulthood vision? If I fail to face inner lightlessness, when I look at the world beyond my prescription frames, do I see through a glass darkly? How did Grandma transform a porch into a classroom and create a timeless space where fears became epiphanies?

On April 6, 2015, my Grandma, Franceina Ellison, exhaled one last time in her ninety-seventh year. As my fingers tap this keyboard and I reflect on lessons learned from her unconventional teaching methods, a swell of grief and deep gratitude washes over me. Prior to her passing, I was less conscious of her deep impression on my own pedagogy. Yet now I stand ruthlessly aware of the manifold ways Grandma's lore frames my teaching in Fearless Dialogues conversations, university classrooms, and sanctuary pulpits. Whether facing fears of country dark, the unknown dread of teenage heartbreak, or the menacing phantoms of institutionalized racism, in her company no issue remained off-limits, no subject was taboo.

Grandma was a top-flight professor, though her formal education ended in high school. To be sure, her method of instruction differed from my faculty mentors at Emory University and Princeton Theological Seminary. Grandma believed that hard conversations rarely emerged in sterile environments, so when I expressed a need to share my truth, something else was always at play. With upturned dirt under our nails, blooming flowers at our knees, and tears in our eyes, we considered the cost of excellence and the isolation of being pedestal-bound. In my college days, she hummed a hymn to calm my nerves, and I felt the warmth of her heart in the boiling pot of soup I stirred. Then I shared with relief, "My HIV test is negative." Decades ago, when terror filled the night, she led me onto a firefly-illumined porch and together we faced my fear of country dark. Grandma mastered the art of creating spaces for discussing life-altering moments.

Creating unique spaces for hard heartfelt conversation is the niche of Fearless Dialogues. As my grandmother intuited, we at Fearless Dialogues believe that authentic and meaningful engagement does not develop by happenstance. Instead, spaces for lasting and transformative dialogue must be crafted with great intentionality. In this chapter, I give you our formula for creating space. Drawing upon Grandma's wisdom, the sacramental vision of Barbara Brown Taylor, and a host of other diverse thinkers, this chapter outlines the three basic principles utilized by Fearless Dialogues to create unique spaces. These three guidelines are:

1. Embrace the possibility of failure.
2. Stimulate the senses.
3. Identify pockets of freedom within the boundaries.

While I could formulaically chart out these three elements, I resist this temptation for two reasons. First, creating unique spaces for penetrating discussion is as much of an art as a science. Given this disciplinary dualism, in these pages you will experience how Fearless Dialogues creates spaces by employing the aesthetic beauty of art and the structured chaos of science. Second, I would do us a disservice to just talk about a space without creating one. So, in the spirit of my grandmother, who took my terror-stricken hand and led me onto a starlit porch, I invite you to journey with me into the country dark.

In these pages, take courage and walk with me beyond the mouth of prehistoric caves. Together, we will squirm on our bellies through tight, damp crevices to uncover how our Paleolithic ancestors transformed their fears of the unknown into life-giving forms of artistic communication. I beckon you to look lovingly at your shadow on our trek through the great outdoors. See your reflection in the rushing stream of consciousness and reckon with the unspoken prejudices looking back at you. Journey with me as we see a science laboratory come to life and we find kinship with the unseen. As we move ever deeper into the country dark, be aware of your fears of the unknown.

Remain cognizant of resistance that has restricted your own speech and frustrated dialogue with those around you. Step with me beyond your luminescent comfort zone and into the pitch where truth comes to light and the enveloping darkness becomes a sacred teacher.

Look back. Now notice the backdraft of moldy air lifting the hairs on your unclothed skin. Hear the cry of large beasts beyond the mouth of our cave ricocheting off the stone walls and trembling in our eardrums. With sharpened rock in one hand and a flickering torch in the other, descend with me into the depths of the cavernous earth.

PALEOLITHIC FEAR: 30,000 YEARS OF CREATING SPACES TO FACE THE UNKNOWN

Lingering in the unconscious mind, the unfamiliar can take on the shape-shifting monstrous form of unknown fear. Rock art in the Paleolithic era proves that such fears of the unknown are woven into human DNA. More than 30,000 years ago, tucked away in womb-like caves,[2] our ancestors painted rock walls and etched into stone their lived reality.[3] While some of these carvings captured real-life renderings of herbivores and human body parts, other drawings illustrated the monstrous forms of potential predators.[4] Left to the fancy of the imagination, these drawings demonstrated the ever-present danger and horrific threats beyond the secure walls of the cave.

Both in the Stone Age and today, fear of the unknown constricts. It clenches the nerves and makes movements measured. It quickens the pulse, heightens awareness, and greets the surrounding world with suspicion and mistrust. In modern parlance, fear of the unknown tightens the jawline, making spoken words more calculated. Indeed, these constrictions prove necessary today for self-protection against identity assault, and in yesteryear the cautionary constrictions were vital to the survival of our species. However, even in the face of clenched nerves and measured movements, our prehistoric progenitors demonstrate that fear of the unknown does not necessarily confine creativity, imprison the imagination, or prevent possibilities of perceptive understanding.

To find sanctuary and solace from the snares of the outside world, our Paleolithic ancestors retreated from the mouths of caves and descended into underground tunnels and dank corridors. Deep in the darkness, where "sights of animal life appeared and disappeared back into the invisible, . . . eerie footsteps and dripping water tickled the ear," and the smell of damp stone settled in the back of the throat, art buttressed life and creativity allayed fears.[5]

Caves were transformative spaces. With rudimentary tools, cave dwellers transformed rock walls into canvases to document internal trauma and process external stimuli. At times, Paleolithic apprentices accompanied master artisans into the deep recesses of the earth, and the stone surfaces became chalkboards for disseminating vital information.[6] Some researchers believe shaman-like priests were selected by prehistoric clans to transform cavernous pits into holy spaces to connect supernaturally with the outer world. In the presence of painted images, archaeologists have even found ancient wind instruments made of vulture bones, suggesting that the chambered walls of the cave could be transformed into a music hall.[7] In sum, thousands of years before we were born, our ancestors created unique spaces for psychological examination, pedagogical formation, spiritual transcendence, and creative exploration. This atypical environment for teaching and cultivation of the self not only lessened fear but also heightened sensory awareness.

In retrospect, my grandmother drew upon the innate resources of our cave-dwelling ancestors. In her wisdom, she transformed a rickety porch in Arkansas into a classroom that titillated my sensory imagination, alerted me to the divine hidden in plain sight, and encouraged me to face my constricting fear of country dark. The Paleolithic cave, the Arkansas porch, and a host of novel learning environments inspired the creation of an unconventional space for hard conversation that I affectionately call the Laboratory of Discovery.

THE LABORATORY OF DISCOVERY:
A MICROSCOPIC LOOK AT CREATING SPACES

For over a decade, I have referred to the unique learning environment that I frame in classroom spaces, church sanctuaries, and community centers as the Laboratory of Discovery. I use the metaphor intentionally because a laboratory, in its best sense, is a place where new knowledge emerges within a controlled environment. Like the scientist, the Fearless Dialogues animator can intentionally control certain elements in the "laboratory," but cannot fully account for the unexpected. Such is the case in a classroom, pulpit, or community conversation. While certain parameters can be put in place to create an optimal environment for discovery to unfold, one cannot fully account for unexpected breakthroughs or breakdowns. In this regard, the animator must be sensitive to the relational dynamics of those in the laboratory, attentive to her own role within these relationships, and fully cognizant of the changing dynamics in the surrounding environment. Ironically, my love of laboratories unfolded more than ten years ago when I realized that I detested science.

In my youth a few well-intentioned mentors and teachers, who noticed critical thinking skills and abiding altruism in me, slowly indoctrinated me into the belief that I should pursue a career as a physician. Having excelled in AP Biology and AP Chemistry, periods of my teenage years were spent volunteering in hospitals and studying the hard sciences in enrichment programs. The summer prior to my junior year in high school, I was chosen as one of thirteen minority students from around the nation to work alongside renowned scientists in a college laboratory. For ten weeks that summer, I donned a starched white lab coat and perforated plastic goggles as an intern in a chemistry laboratory at Spelman College.

That summer I filled my days mixing chemicals, learning physics, and memorizing combinations of elements from the periodic table. Though I could not articulate it with my mouth, I knew in my heart that I lacked the passion to pursue a career in the sciences. This sense was confirmed a few years later when I landed on academic probation after earning a D– in freshman chemistry at Emory. Yet I fought through my dispassion of the subject because of the multisensory allure of laboratory life.

Everything about the laboratory stimulated me. I remember those days in my Spelman College lab coat like yesterday. Captivated by color and shape, I recall gazing for nearly an hour at a boiling yellow greenish liquid in a crystal clear oblong beaker. Cast over the Bunsen burner, my nostrils deciphered the pungent gas from the blue-orange flame, but the scent from the bubbling liquid stumped my olfactory system. All the while, the spinning centrifuge hummed a few octaves higher than the fridge cooling the covered petri dishes. Enthralled by the lab, on occasion I skipped lunch breaks to sketch the lined shelves of beakers, statuesque microscopes, and shiny ebony countertops in my composition book.

In retrospect, the science of the laboratory stood secondary to the creative energy that it generated in me. The shared community of innovators, with both their openness to failure and their expectation of breakthrough, pushed me to probe deeply and think broadly. The panoply of color, tantalizing smells, and cacophonous sound jolted my imagination. In this space of discovery, I breathed more deeply, and my heart pumped stronger, because the laboratory was alive. That summer as a lab tech left such an indelible mark on me that for years I sought spaces that could mirror what I saw in my reflection on that ebony countertop.

After experiencing my freshman chemistry debacle and discerning my gifts as a teacher, I changed my major to religion and sociology. During this process of discernment, I experimented with full-sensory pedagogies. In classrooms, community centers, and Bible studies, I mixed elements from Grandma's teaching and theories learned in my university courses with art, music, and the folk wisdom of city streets. At times this concoction of pedagogies blew up in my face. In other instances, I witnessed piqued imaginations, heightened consciousness, and vitalized minds. After years of mixing and matching, these distinct teaching elements were topspun in the centrifuge of my soul, and a crystalline space of learning formed called the Laboratory of Discovery. The uniquely created space in the Laboratory of Discovery, much like the classroom my grandmother crafted on the porch and the safe havens our Paleolithic progenitors configured in caves, consists of three key elements:

1. Embracing the unknown to forge gateways of discovery
2. Stimulating the senses to awaken the imagination
3. Engaging the ecosystem to transform seeing, hearing, and knowing

In the following pages, I microscopically observe and meticulously dissect each of these three principles that are central to creating the unique spaces reflected in the work of Fearless Dialogues.

THE UNKNOWN AS HOLY MYSTERY: EMBRACING THE BRIGHT CLOUD OF UNKNOWING

Imagine. The sun has not yet risen, and you find yourself driving alone on a winding mountain road. You bend your vehicle around each curve with great caution, fully aware that one wrong turn could send you tumbling over the three-foot guardrail. "What is the purpose of a three-foot guardrail anyway?" your mind wonders. As the sun begins to break on the distant horizon, you angle your wheel around a blind curve, and immediately a thick and ominous fog blankets your windshield. At a snail's pace, your tires inch up the mountain. With your eyes fixed on the dotted line, you give thanks for the bright yellow guardrail. As you move ever deeper into the fog, chill bumps stand like legions on your arm. With every trepidatious tire spin, your mind cycles through fear-inducing memories: the rainy day spin-out you witnessed weeks ago on your morning commute, the thick and blinding smoke of your neighbor's burning home, yesterday's headline news of the plane crashing in inclement weather. In the thicket of memory-induced fright, you notice the presence of the breaking sun and again offer thanks. You are in the fog, and in your fear. Yet you bravely inch forward into the unknown.

When community leaders enter into Fearless Dialogues spaces, every step toward conversation may feel like driving into a mountainous fog. The partners gathered for dialogue are likely aware that our team has been invited to create an environment for hard conversation about some pressing issue that remains unspoken in their community. Therefore, each movement closer to dialogue may trigger mystery, suspicion, and even dread. Sly smiles may cover haunting memories. Forced laughter may conceal nervous energy about saying something that could offend others or vilify oneself. But animators recognize that there is courage in showing up. By their mere presence, even the most aloof person fearlessly inches toward dialogue. While it is impossible to psychoanalyze each individual and determine how their unknown fears are being projected on the landscape of discussion, it is possible to create an environment where those gathered move forward in reverence and awe of unsighted clearings that may lie around the bend.

Episcopal priest, university professor, and internationally praised writer Barbara Brown Taylor navigates through the brume of biblical interpretation and recounts another harrowing mountaintop experience that has befuddled Bible readers for ages. Reflecting on Matthew 17:1–9, Taylor draws us into the world of Peter, James, and John as they embark on a "long climb up a windy mountain [with Jesus] in the fading light of day."[8] In their search for solace and a space to pray, Jesus is transfigured before them. "Jesus, someone you thought you knew well, standing there pulsing with light. . . . Face like a flame. Then, as if that weren't enough, two other people are there with him, all of them standing in that same bright light, . . . Moses. Elijah. Dead men come back to life. God's own glory lighting up the night."[9] Enveloped by light in the midst of mountainous darkness, Peter utters a few words. But before Peter can punctuate the end of his thought, "a terrifying cloud that is also alive" rolls in and stammers his tongue. Surrounded by the cloud and constricted by a fear of the unknown, Peter, James, and John forget the luminous three and fall face down in speechless terror.

In the first line of Taylor's appropriately titled sermon "The Bright Cloud of Unknowing," she proclaims that the transfiguration story "defies interpretation, although that has not stopped legions of interpreters from trying."[10] Resisting the homiletical impulse to discern the content of the story and place it neatly before the hearer, Taylor posits, "What if the point is not to decode the cloud but to enter it? What if the whole Bible is less a book of certainties than it is a book of encounters?" In such encounters people walk unwittingly into the unknown, then "run into God, each other, and life—and are never the same again."[11]

For Taylor, biblical encounters break people open and rearrange what they think they know for sure, so that there is room for divine movement in their lives.[12] In some instances the movement of encounter mandates travel from one place to another. But in other instances the movement is an internal journey from head to heart. "Certainties become casualties" in divine encounters. Inside the bright cloud of unknowing, the unknown has the potential to become a gift—if we can become fully present to what is happening right in front of us, rather than being certain of what it all means.

The Laboratory of Discovery embraces unknowing, so that people can run into themselves and the unlikely partners around them. These divine encounters emerge when unlikely partners acknowledge their fears, lay down the need for certainty, and become fully present to unfolding possibilities before them. Yet facing hard problems in the company of unlikely partners is a steep climb up mountainous terrain. Before unlikely partners enter the space of conversation, Fearless Dialogues animators pray for open minds, open hearts, and the presence of ancestral luminaries to transform fear into divine encounter.

By the time unlikely partners set foot in the space, Fearless Dialogues animators are embodying Radical Hospitality (discussed in the following chapter) to serve as guardrails around difficult bends. During heated and emotive conversation, unlikely partners are encouraged to trust their inner guide and strain to recall moments when hard conversations led to the dawning of hope on the horizon. With each cautious step into dialogue, unlikely partners forestall unknown fears and bravely trust that they will encounter anew the world in them and around them. But, why trust in animators whom one barely knows, or put faith in a process that at first glance looks as clear as pea soup on a mountain slope?

Facing fear, relinquishing certainty, and grounding oneself in the present require a trust in animators that cannot be earned in just a few moments. So we build rapport with the past by evoking memories. In creating spaces for hard conversation, Fearless Dialogues animators foster trust by piquing the curiosity of those gathered and suggesting that undiscovered solutions lie dormant in the room. With some convincing, we propose that invoking the imagination can transport one from the seemingly intractable terrain of the taboo into a wondrous world of solutions. Too good to be true, you say? Open your mind.

> *imagine.*
> *dream.*
> *remember.*

THE UNKNOWN AS FAMILIAR: REIGNITING IMAGINATION TO SEE ANEW

Reminding me of the night terrors of my own youth, my six-year-old daughter often wrestles with her bed sheets at night as fanciful dreams paint pictures in her subconscious. On one particular Sunday evening, a soprano-pitched "Daddy" pierces the midnight calm. I groggily labor down the hall. True to form, her ballerina bedding is disheveled, and her stuffed pink unicorn lies at the foot of the bed. As I enter the bedroom, her alerted eyes convey confusion, not horror. "My tooth that you pulled is not under my pillow anymore. But the tooth fairy didn't leave any money. Do you think she forgot?" After a wildly creative response of my own—to avoid spoiling her fantasy—I rewrap my daughter in her whirlwind of ballerina sheets, snuggle her close to her pink unicorn, and pray that she returns to the playful dreamland of the winged tooth fairy.

Just as my grandmother led me on to a candlelit porch to expose me to the wonders of country dark, I tuck my own daughter under taut sheets next to her stuffed single-horned horse, in the hopes of creating an atmosphere for curiosity and creativity. Operating under the belief that an atmosphere of openness invites novel thinking and courageous conversation, Fearless Dialogues creates similar spaces for the imagination to wander. However, for some unlikely partners, the shelf life of their imagination reads expired. For these, the childhood wiles of curiosity and creativity are tossed aside in favor of the adult "virtues" of utility, reason, and productivity. How then does Fearless Dialogues rekindle the imagination and ignite a fervor for seeing, hearing, and knowing differently? We invite unlikely partners to return to their childhood.

Remember the moment when you lost your imagination? On one day, you raced metal Matchbox cars across the floor. You could smell the rubber from screeching tires, and from the depths of your belly you belched out sounds like "Vroom!" and "Zoom!" Perhaps on that day you lined your dolls along the wall, and mimicking your first-grade teacher, you read to your assembled class, "I do not like green eggs and ham. I do not, like them, Sam-I-am."[13] Sure, you stumbled over words you just learned, but in your ears the readings sounded eloquent and the transfixed eyes of your students affirmed as much. Then one day something changed. You pushed the metal car across the floor, but the engine sound did not leave your throat. You read aloud to your assembled class, but your students' faces looked like dolls with blank stares. "A world that had been plump with meaning had suddenly become flat and one-dimensional."[14] *Where had your imagination gone?*

Following the lead of Barbara Brown Taylor, who believes that "the church's central task is an imaginative one," I believe that a primary role of Fearless Dialogues is to restoke the fire of imagination. For Taylor, the imaginative task is not fanciful or fictional. Instead, the human capacity to imagine enables us to form mental pictures of our self, our neighbor, our world, and our future. This ability to envision new realities engages and transforms. To remind us that everyone has the gift of imagination, Taylor highlights the virtuosity of small children whose minds have not yet been constrained by "realities" of adulthood. Part of children's secrets to exploring new vistas with their minds, she explains, is a natural ability to employ all of their senses.[15]

> Small children have not yet learned to view the world around them as scenery, a flat backdrop to walk past on their way to somewhere else. They are still immersed in it, up to their eyes in colors, up to their ears in sounds, with fingertips that ache to stroke a sparrow and noses that can find a creek in the dark by its smell. They live in a world where sharp distinctions need not be made, where green is a texture as well as a hue, where rain has a taste as important as its temperature, where the sound of sunlight can be deafening at noon. . . . Their imagination thrives on the sensual details that their elders have learned to take for granted.[16]

Guided by a wise sage, my childhood senses were ignited on an Arkansas porch, and the fires of my sensory memory were rekindled in that Spelman laboratory. The boiling beaker and the spinning centrifuge echoed the cricket chorus and the whir of the twirling ice-cream tin. Though I could no longer hear the tire screech of Matchbox cars in my lab-coated teenage years, my imagination was enlivened in a controlled space. Fearless Dialogues creates similar spaces to titillate the senses of adults and to awaken dormant imaginations. But to do so, more learning of how children perceive the world is required.

Taylor acknowledges that another gift of children's imagination is their lack of awareness of what things are to be and how adults believe that they should be used. For instance, she shares that, while adults may use a comb solely for their hair, a child might use this fine-toothed tool as a musical instrument, a back scratcher, or a device to carve out racetracks for ants.[17] The wandering imaginative minds of children are full of fascination, uncertainty, and endless possibility—all lessons from which we their older counterparts can learn, if we seek to see ourselves and the world anew.

Believing that seeing the world with wonder can teach adults to engage with God and neighbor differently, Taylor advocates for an apprenticeship to children and a study of their imaginative outlook. While my grandmother was indeed a master teacher, what sparkle did she see in my six-year-old eyes, as the stars and fireflies came alive in the country dark? Taylor suggests that entering into a child's imaginative world teaches adults to surrender certainty, assume nothing, and come to approach every created thing with awe.[18] Such apprenticeship, if only for a few moments, triggers a recovery of what we once knew in our youth, but have forgotten with time.

In Fearless Dialogues community conversations, we intentionally create spaces for unlikely partners to imaginatively apprentice with their childhood self in hope of recovering the vestiges of their once boundless imaginations. As unlikely partners enter the space, they are greeted by an experiment we call the Living Museum. In hypnotic fashion, a Fearless Dialogues animator serves as a curator for the exhibit and invites the unlikely partners to gather in small groups of five or six. Standing before the small cadre of leaders, the curator might say something like this:

> Welcome to the Living Museum. Beyond these doors is something far different than the fine galleries of art in your city center. This

museum breathes and talks, and challenges us to remember. Outside of these doors you will find members of the Fearless Dialogues team standing on chairs and holding photographs and paintings of children and teenagers from around the globe. Our team is standing on chairs and holding these images at waist length, so that as you walk through the Living Museum you can look these young people in the eye. Did I mention this is no ordinary museum? I challenge you not to look at the images flatly or abstractly. Instead, I call you to remember. As you look into the eyes of the image, recall someone in your life whom the pictured person represents. Their skin color may be different, their clothes may be tattered; but whom does this person staring back at you remind you of? Is it someone from your high school, your office, your church, your family? Is it you? And as you ponder these questions, my colleagues standing in the chairs have three questions for you to answer aloud: Who do you see? Who don't you hear? Where is hope? You may also ask questions of our team members standing in those chairs, for they have heard the responses of other members of your community. See. Hear. Remember. Welcome to the Living Museum.

At every venue, we open the Living Museum with a picture of a fair-skinned black boy three years of age. Donning a green velvet coat and yellow bow tie, the child sits in a white art-deco chair with eyes upturned; he holds a globe above his head. As the unlikely partners gather around the image, I often observe their eyes lifting toward the ceiling; perhaps in this upward gaze they unconsciously recount the hopes of their childhood. Transfixed, they search through the annals of their memory, as if they were flipping through an old-school Rolodex to find the appropriate face and name of whoever the child represents. In a community conversation with former gang leaders in New Orleans, I recall one unlikely partner saying, "This little boy looks like he's ready to take on the world. I don't see many like him where I'm from. Is he black?" At another community conversation with corporate leaders in Atlanta, a wealthy white woman stood spellbound by the bow-tied boy's gaze: "The life in his eyes reminds me of the children I met many years ago in South America." After this comment she stood in a retrospective silence as the other four in her small group also brought the image to life with their memories.

In the Living Museum the former gang leader, the corporate executive, and the unlikely partners who gather around provocative images find their imaginations leading them to unknown spaces. Before the adulthood objection, "Why should I share personal memories in mixed company?" kicks in, the strong pull of imagination draws unlikely partners into intimate conversation with a small group of strangers. For this reason, we call the Living Museum "the conversation before the conversation." Without firm consciousness of what is actually happening, unlikely partners who may have been ridden with anxiety just minutes earlier courageously share private truths. This initial exercise of imaginative play subversively draws into the room parts of the self that were not expected to enter, leaving the gang leader questioning, "What does this have to do with community violence?" and the executive wondering, "I thought this session was about corporate accountability and business ethics." As the unlikely partners come to see Rolodexed faces in their minds, they are primed to imagine the faces and lived realities of others whose stories differ from theirs. I speak of this interplay of imagination and empathy for strangers in the next chapter. In short, Fearless Dialogues harnesses the imagination to expand the vantage point of the participant, open their mind to whimsy, and draw into the dialogue a cloud of witnesses not physically present.

THE UNKNOWN AS UNIFIED SPACE: LESSONS FROM A LIVING ECOSYSTEM

For over three decades, my soles tramped upon Georgia red clay. But never before had my soul trod on Peruvian soil. Or so I thought . . .

Though the landscape of my interior is a vast dream world, prior to 2012 my passport bore a single stamp, from a honeymoon trip to Jamaica. In August 2012, a faculty colleague leading a travel seminar fell ill, and as a substitute teacher of sorts, I earned passport stamp number two. Along with a delegation of Candler School of Theology students and religious leaders, I traveled to the World Methodist Evangelism Institute in Peru. As waves crashed upon the Peruvian shores at the beachfront conference center, dozens of seminarians, ministers, bishops, and laypersons from Bolivia, Colombia, Brazil, and Peru hashed out the new face of missions in Central and South America. Come Sunday morning, teams of ministers were dispatched throughout the country to worship. Our group was sent to the country's capital, Lima.

To my surprise, upon arrival at the Methodist church in the city's center, I was escorted to the pulpit to preach. As I stood behind the holy lectern, I paused for several minutes and looked into the eyes of the congregants gathered. Captivated by the faces before me, I noticed my brow furl. With my head angled to the right in confusion, a passing thought raced through my body: "I've never been to Lima, but I've seen these people before." Repressing my confusion, with the aid of a translator I offered my customary greeting, "It is good to finally see you. . . . Our text for this morning is . . ." Thirty minutes later, I stood at the exit to greet the congregants filing out of the church. After several hugs, smiles, and translated courtesies, a middle-aged man in ruddy work clothes approached me with open arms. His face was strangely familiar, and when he spoke, I recognized his voice. "It is good to see you again, Greg." Time froze. We met in a dream.

The world we live in is interconnected. All creation—animate and inanimate, physical and metaphysical—operates in a vastly mysterious ecosystem. Since my encounter in Peru, I have wrestled with the boundless unknown on one hand, and the multidimensionality of space on the other. Three books altered how I move in the world and informed how Fearless Dialogues embraces entire ecosystems to create spaces for individual and communal healing: Barbara Brown Taylor's *An Altar in the World*, Steve de Shazer's *Patterns of Brief Therapy*, and Ayi Kwei Armah's *The Healers*. While I examine de Shazer's work in my first book, and I hope to explore Armah's African cosmology in future research, I devote the final pages of this chapter to Taylor's *An Altar in the World*. Chief among my learnings from these books is the necessity to decenter myself from the universe, and to attend to the world of which I am a part (and not the whole). By guiding participants to see the whole and to revere its parts, Fearless Dialogues cultivates a seeing that combats invisibility and muteness.

SEEING THE WORLD WITH REVERENCE

One of the ten most formative books I have ever read, Barbara Brown Taylor's *An Altar in the World* presents a dozen practices that can reveal the Divine in everyday life. A trained Episcopal priest with the mystical eye of a wise sage, Taylor argues that "[if] regarded properly, anything can become a sacrament, by [sacrament, she] means an outward visible sign of an inward spiritual connection."[19] Page after page, through biographic narratives and historical accounts, Taylor invites readers to find sacramental wisdom and spiritual meaning in seemingly mundane tasks like walking,[20] washing clothes,[21] making chicken salad,[22] and shaking hands.[23] I found the practice of paying attention and its complementary virtue of reverence most compelling and convicting, as I tussled with my Peruvian encounter and the interconnectedness of the world around me.

As the child of a military veteran, in her youth Taylor learned timeless lessons about reverence from her father. Daddy Brown was not your everyday churchgoer, so reverence had "nothing to do with religion and very little to do with God."[24] Instead, through his soldiered eyes, reverence had more to do with "knowing your rank in the overall scheme of things."[25] In his mind, reverence required a proper attitude of positioning yourself in a vast world occupied by fascinating people, places, and things. Under his tutelage and paternal example, Taylor learned that a proper reverential attitude was warranted in all situations, whether one was walking through a starlit forest, bandaging an open wound, or meticulously cleaning the chamber of a hunter's rifle. In every instance, the reverent one must pay attention, take care, respect things that can kill you, and make the passage from fear to awe.[26] But as the soldier's daughter would learn, developing a reverent eye takes time and, for that matter, requires a certain pace.

Really paying attention to the wondrous possibilities for insight all around us takes time. Slowing down does not necessarily mean stopping to gaze at every flower, using one's lunch break to people watch, or spending every night marveling at the sunset. While each of these practices might make for a lower heart rate, in a frenzied world of work deadlines and cell-phone reminders, completely stopping for many seems unrealistic. However, instead of walking sixty steps per minute, one might walk forty-five. With a slight alteration in pace, consciousness overrides ritual; the mind awakens; detours lead to clearings; and clarity creates even more sought-after detours.

At Fearless Dialogues we create environments that shave off fifteen steps so that unlikely partners who customarily move at breakneck speed may begin to see the world anew. For example, once the unlikely partners gather for the first time in a single room, before the lead animator offers a single word, he or she care+fully and wondrously looks each individual in the eye. After taking time to see every person, who may have previously felt invisible, the lead animator cracks the quiet with seven words: "It is good to finally see you." I will say more about this greeting later in this section, but taking a pregnant pause to behold with awe lowers the collective heart rate, decreases the pace to forty-five steps per minute, and prepares the assembled interlocutors to perceive differently. Slowing down to see also requires the courage to fear+lessly face the unknown world that cannot be glimpsed by rapid glances.

Taylor describes the great outdoors much like a laboratory of discovery designed by God to teach us reverence. But as a chemist leans over a microscope primed for discovery or disaster, in nature's laboratory the reverent observer must be unafraid of being mystified by matters of creation that dwarf the self and befuddle human understanding. With your imaginary lab coat, walk into the great outdoors and field test your reverential vision. Take care as you step over holes in the desert, lest a rattlesnake greet you unawares. Understand that in a cornfield the expanse of light before the roll of thunder can kill you. As you pay attention to the cricket's song and the lightning bug's beacon, marvel at your kinship with the salt marsh mosquito feasting on your arm, and the soul of the solitary pebble tossed in the rushing river. Reverential regard in nature uncovers untold interconnections with the animate and inanimate alike. However, as Taylor duly notes, reverencing nature comes fairly easy for many, but showing reverence for people presents a greater challenge.[27]

Helping unlikely partners to reverence, to take care, and to pay attention to their kinship with *all* people is the sacramental task of Fearless Dialogues. Taylor cautions that the "irreverent soul who is unable to feel awe in things higher than the self is also unable to feel respect in the presence of things it sees as lower than the self."[28] Many of the unlikely partners who gather at Fearless Dialogues conversations would surely not label their souls as irreverent. After all, most of the persons who gather for these community conversations hold a baseline respect for God, creation, and the well-being of the world. Yet, does a subconscious disdain linger for those seen as lower than oneself? Do the homeless hordes on city streets, the meth heads with missing teeth, the dope boys with sagging pants, and the 1 percent in Lear jets, turn stomachs, create sour tastes, and make blood boil?

Using interactive exercises like the Three-Feet Challenge (discussed in chapter 1), Strange Freedom (chapter 4), the Five Hardest Questions (chapter 5), or the Long Loving Look at the Real (chapter 5), Fearless Dialogues animators put a finger on the irreverence often shown to the unacknowledged. Then, with soldiered eyes, these trained animators remind unlikely partners that our destinies are interwoven with the least of these.

In the uniquely created spaces of Fearless Dialogues, unlikely partners practice reverence by reckoning with the unexcavated contempt, unearthed disgust, and ungouged prejudice for those who share the earth with us. Like the military father with his wide-eyed daughter, Fearless Dialogues animators carefully walk at a measured pace with unlikely partners into the dense forests of unconscious bias. Once surrounded by all matters of creation that inspire awe and befuddle understanding, we pose a question during the Living Museum: Who do you see?

This question casts a net for reverent responses that accompany unlikely partners down their streams of consciousness: Is the child staring back at you in the picture worthy of your attention? Is the person standing beside you, and listening for your words, deserving of your care? In the eyes of the person seated before you, can you glimpse the holy of holies? With each probing question, the Fearless Dialogues Laboratory of Discovery scratches the subconscious and creates a space to see with wonder and reverence. With clear eyes to see the unknown with reverence and awe, the next hurdle to leap on the track for social change is overcoming the fear of strangers.

A FINAL WORD
FUNKJAZZ KAFE AND THE ART OF FRAMING SPACE

As nightfall blackened the summer sky, a spectacle of colors awakened Atlanta's cityscape. Standing on the corner of Spring and Luckie, a person with a careful eye could catch the reflective beams of top-lit sky-scrapers dancing on the Tabernacle's vibrating stained glass. When the red-bricked neoclassical Baptist Tabernacle opened its doors in March 1911, more than eight thousand Victorian-suited men and corseted women stood on the same corner waiting to worship in the sprawling auditorium with two balconies.[29]

However, on July 13, 2013, as hundreds lined the city streets donned for a nightlife experience like none other, souls would be moved in a different fashion. My wife and I stood among the throng counting down the minutes until the doors swung open. Then cutting through the crowd and seemingly gliding through the air, a Chakaba stilt walker hovered ten feet above the ground waving a flag.[30] Like the kaleidoscopic colors on the building's paned glass, the Chakaba's sequined outfit spangled in the night, and as if calling from the heavens, he yelled out, "Y'all ready? Welcome to FunkJazz Kafe!" The doors swung open, the crowd ascended the stairs, filed through the arched doorways, and entered into an unknown world of artistic expression.

The brainchild of Atlanta native Jason Orr, FunkJazz Kafe creates spaces for a one-of-a-kind cultural arts extravaganza. Under one roof, a ticketholder can observe a sculptor fashioning clay and an oil painter bringing a canvas to life. She can taste vegetarian-based Jamaican cuisine and feel the flavor of Brazilian capoeira artists. At FunkJazz Kafe, you can hear live music from an undiscovered voice from "across the pond," or feel the rafters shaking as the dancing crowd sings along with a Grammy-winning artist. The novelty of this cultural bazaar is that thousands of tickets are sold, yet prior to the ticketholder's entry into FunkJazz Kafe, the visual and vocal artists to perform are unknown.

On that July evening, an ecosystem was created where visual art came to life, savory food smells filled the air, and souls diverse in age and background gathered under the FunkJazz banner. Antoinette and I were seated in the balcony when Big Boi, one half of Atlanta's chart-busting duo Outkast, took the stage. The crowd erupted, yet before the beat dropped for his rhyme, he shared with the captive audience that just minutes earlier George Zimmerman, the killer of Trayvon Martin, had been found not guilty.

Discontented, yet cradled in an ecosystem of art and innovation, at that moment I began to dream of how our first Fearless Dialogues Community Conversation the following week should unfold. Imagination took flight. I began to dream. Like the FunkJazz stilt walkers, Fearless Dialogues animators would welcome unlikely partners into the Laboratory of Discovery and invite them to embrace the unknown. We too would creatively use art, music, and food to stoke the imagination and transform the environment from a place of contentious debate to a living ecosystem for truth sharing. By the end of that first Fearless Dialogues conversation a week after FunkJazz Kafe, our team learned that creating space for truth telling requires far more than embracing failure, stimulating the senses, and enlivening the ecosystem. Hard heartfelt conversation with unlikely partners rarely unfolds unless the company of strangers are welcomed with Radical Hospitality and made to feel at home.

3

The Welcome Table of Radical Hospitality

Beyond the Fear of Strangers

Them bright yella eggs in the cast-iron skillet always reminded me of the sun cuttin' through the midnight sky. But, it was mornin' in Granma's house, breakfast was cookin', and the usuals were startin' to gather. Some kinda meat simmered in a skillet next to the eggs. 'Possum? Rabbit? Squirl? All tasted the same to me when they was fried and smothered in gravy. On the back burner, a golden river of butter ran through the bubblin' stone ground grits like the "ancient, dusky" Mississippi.[1]

Under the eggs, mystery meat, and boiling grits, the heat from the oven pushed the air out the dough, and homemade biscuits the size of my eight-year-old hand was risin' like white clouds in the sky. Molasses sat on the table next to the canned pear preserves, and every thirty seconds the screen door was a-slammin' as folk kept filing in to 135 Webster.

Eatin' was sport for my family. And folk came from miles away, like countries gathering for the torch lighting of the Olympic Games, just to put they feet under Granma's table. Of course the usuals were there. Granpa and Uncle Jack in their uniformed denim coveralls took their seats at the big table. Not long after, Uncle Slim and Aunt LC moseyed in. The Saddlers thundered up the back steps, and like a songbird in springtime cousin Tweety came a-hummin' through the front door. In piccolo pitch, Aunt Lela sent her greetings to everybody, and kids upon kids upon kids scurried for an empty spot to

fill their mornin' bellies. After a customary prayer, we all grabbed our
platter—'cause sport eaters don't use plates—and the games began.

It took years for me to appreciate the subtle lessons of warm reception that I learned at 135 Webster. On any given day, Granma could
feed twenty to fifty people. My grandparents were far from wealthy,
but as migrants from the Mississippi cotton fields they opened their
table to all, and no one ever walked away hungry.

Granma was the oldest of eighteen children, and Granpa was number four of twelve. Because our clan was so large, and I didn't know
half the folk milling around the tables, I figured they was all family.
I have since learned that many of the diners weren't related, but my
grandparents still treated them like kin. The sojourners from the block
came in through the screen door, washed their hands, and ate off their
platter with everybody else.

After the morning rush, Granma and Granpa sat on the front porch
and "chewed the fat." Leftovers stayed on the stove until the next meal.
If by chance they saw an empty-stomached sojourner walk by, the
screen door would slam again, the hungry pedestrian would wash her
hands, and sit at the welcome table.

As comforting as a mother's hug, the food prepared in Granma's kitchen
put souls at ease. Around platters of piping hot grits, cathead biscuits,
and all manner of mystery meats, family, friend, and foe let down their
walls, removed their masks, and spoke their mind without inhibition.
Around those tables food for thought was served buffet style, as heartfelt conversations on politics and parenting, faith and activism, history
and current events unfolded effortlessly.

Not much on words, Granma Simpson was the quiet type. Interestingly, while others ate, she rarely took a bite. She retreated to her recliner
in the corner to "rest." If ever questioned about her appetite, Granma
responded, "Baby, I'm tired. I'll eat lil' later." But her lively eyes told a
different story. Amid the chatter and the chew, she scanned the room,
processing data. She looked and listened, learned and laughed. With
her long loving looks, she took in the minute details that others overlooked. Quite often Granma's eyes would connect with a diner, and in
minutes the full-bellied partaker would saunter to the corner and sit at
her side. Barely above a whisper, diner after diner would disclose deep
and intimate truths to Granma. With a few carefully chosen words, she
would top off their meal with wise counsel.

On June 25, 2007, my Granma, Mary Jane Simpson, exhaled one last time in her eighty-second year. Prior to her death, she invited me to offer words of comfort and encouragement at her funeral. In preparation for Granma's eulogy, I polled family and friends, inquiring of her impact. She was most remembered for her down-home cooking, her wise counsel, and her capacity to hold a confidence with lock and key. On the day of her homegoing celebration, I stood before the hundreds gathered and emphasized five key words: "Granma never met a stranger."

In this chapter, I draw upon the sage-like wisdom of Granma Simpson, Henri Nouwen, Parker J. Palmer, and others, to share with you how Fearless Dialogues engages a fourfold method of Radical Hospitality to sidestep our perilous fear of strangers. To frame these spaces of Radical Hospitality, Fearless Dialogues:

1. Incorporates placeholders that evoke memories of communal solidarity;
2. Models the act of beholding to foster unspoken bonds of social responsibility;
3. Fashions a homelike holding environment for guests to feel secure; and
4. Ensures the host prepares to welcome others long before guests arrive.

With a commitment to intentionally facing fears and innovatively invoking the whole self, Fearless Dialogues transforms unlikely partners into strangers no more.

THE COMPANY OF STRANGERS: HOSPITALITY, HOSTILITY, AND THE FEARS OF LOVING THY NEIGHBOR

From childhood many of us are taught to fear strangers. We are schooled to believe that those unknown to parents and guardians should automatically be looked at askew and arouse skepticism. These socialized suspicions subliminally teach us that those in our inner circle, who look, talk, dress, and think like us, should be perceived as less of a threat. Youthful recollections of "stranger danger" fester for years and unconsciously seep into adulthood interactions, precluding hard heartfelt conversations and meaningful interactions. From these childhood teachings, difference and otherness far too often evoke, and are equated with, fear.

Recognizing that fear of strangers can imperil dialogue and meaningful encounter with others, I invite you to consider four types of strangers that linger in our midst: Public Strangers, Familiar Strangers, Intimate Strangers, and the Stranger Within.[2] Each of these strangers bears gifts that can teach us much about ourselves and the world around us, if we can move from hostility to hospitality and muster the courage to face strangers fear+lessly. But, as I learned in my youth, hospitality is exhausting work.

While Granma and Granpa's residence served as a family hub in the Midwest, my parents' home, affectionately known as the Do Drop Inn, was the southernmost family junction. For Grandma Franceina, the snowbird, our Atlanta home was an annual haven from the wintry mix of ice and snow in the Show-Me state. For cousin Damon, the pilot, our home was a layover pad to rest between flights. For cousins Tina, Audrey, Leslie, Aaron, Neil, and all of their collegiate friends, our home doubled as a free laundromat with the perks of comfortable sofas for napping and foil-wrapped care packages of fried chicken and peach cobbler. For more than one relative, our home served as a rent-free stopgap between jobs and relationships, all manner of personal crises. Throughout my childhood and teenage years, family members, friends, and even friends of friends moved in and out of our abode as if it had a revolving door. All the while, my mother, father, brother, and I learned to shift the equilibrium of our daily routine in order for strangers to feel welcomed in our home.

Such shifts in the interests of hospitality did not come without sacrifice and searing discontent. Mom bemoaned the fact that our house never stayed clean more than a couple of hours. Dad, an accountant and a good steward of our family funds, had no problem playing "bad cop" and setting arrival and departure dates for guests. My younger brother, DE, bellyached about visitors overstaying their welcome. I begrudgingly surrendered my bed to older relatives. In one such surrendering, I slept on a sofa most of my junior year in high school. As one of the innkeepers at the Do Drop Inn, I learned that, if left unchecked, constantly welcoming strangers could breed repulsion and hostility rather than Radical Hospitality.

In *Reaching Out: Three Movements of the Spiritual Life*, Henri Nouwen recognizes the hosts' ambivalence toward strangers and the dutiful work required to create a hospitable environment for unfamiliar people to share freely of themselves. The potential for hostility never escapes the host. Nouwen, like my Granma and innkeeping parents, understood hospitality as a spiritual imperative for Christian living, with age-old roots in the Old and New Testaments.

Far from "the image of soft sweet kindness" or "a general atmosphere of coziness," countless biblical texts reference the sacrifice, risk, and reward of sheltering strangers.[3] Abraham and Sarah offer water, shelter, and their finest meal to three sojourners trekking through Mamre in the heat of the day. A woman named Rahab, who is employed as a prostitute, accepts great risk to herself and her family by protecting Israelite spies from the soldiers sent by the king of Jericho. Two wayfarers encounter a stranger on the road to Emmaus and invite him to a shared meal and shelter, only to find that the stranger is Jesus! In each of these scriptural passages, the hosts welcome unfamiliar persons into the sacred spaces of their homes, unaware of the rewards and despite the risks. In these sacred texts, Abraham, Sarah, and the Emmaus wayfarers sacrifice time, energy, and hard-earned resources to offer a welcome table of food and drink to strangers on their journey. Others, like Rahab, risk their lives and livelihood to shelter the strangers whom others avoid.

From these biblical accounts Nouwen suggests that spaces of hospitality create unique moments where both "guest and host can reveal their most precious gifts and bring new life to each other."[4] Perhaps Nouwen's mentee Parker Palmer is correct when he suggests that strangers bear a truth and vision that may not be revealed without the hospitality of an open-minded host.[5] In a world desperately in need of neighborliness, welcome, and life-altering truths, reclaiming hospitality is necessary. However, reclaiming a form of hospitality that moves from mere kindness to sacrifice and risk requires deep investment and preparation of the host.

A host who seats guests solely to receive the gifts of new vision and the rewards of new truth is little more than a paternalistic maître d' feeding his or her ego. To the contrary, hosts must prepare their inner lives prior to the stranger's arrival, lest they greet the visitor with self-interest, paternalism, hostility, or angst. Upon reflecting on these scriptural passages, examining numerous theories, and observing the conditions necessary for host and stranger to share gifts in mutuality, I have devised an approach called Radical Hospitality to govern the practices of Fearless Dialogues.

To account for the variety of guests gathering for heartfelt conversation, Fearless Dialogues' Radical Hospitality ensures that:

1. Public Strangers are presented placeholders that transition their souls to a space of comfort where truths are revealed and gifts are shared.
2. Familiar Strangers are invited to behold self and others with contemplative eyes.
3. Intimate Strangers are welcomed into an environment that holds them in the crucible of crisis.
4. The host moves toward facing the Stranger Within.

Each of the radically hospitable acts—placeholding, beholding, holding, and moving—sets the table for life-altering encounters and unforgettable moments of Fearless Dialogue. For starters, let me introduce you to the Public Strangers all around us.

PUBLIC STRANGERS: PRECIOUS MEMORIES AND PUBLIC WITNESS

Theirs is a story as American as Huckleberry Finn, as patriotic as Susan B. Anthony. Born in the second decade of the twentieth century, the broader public expected Mary Jane Young and Willie "Dub" Simpson to live the fullness of their lives tilling the blood-soaked soil of a land not their own. This was not a far-fetched prediction. Their mothers and their mothers' mothers, their fathers and their father's fathers, had all picked cotton in the sticky heat of the Mississippi sun. So too the pair were pupils of the Great Depression and schooled in the ways of the Jim Crow South. With Dub formally educated only through fourth grade, and Mary Jane making it only to grade eight, it would seem the generational trend of sharecropping white folks' land would continue for the childhood sweethearts. Days after their betrothal they vowed, "All our kids will go to college. None of them will pick a piece of cotton."

One day, after years of degradation, Dub struck the white landowner. With a bounty on his life, the couple sought "the warmth of other suns."[6] Trudging clandestinely up the Delta, they found solace in a sleepy midwestern manufacturing town. In the company of strangers, they set up shop. They were faithful to their vow; years later, each of their eleven children went to college. Not a single one felt the thorny prick of a Mississippi cotton plant. This classic tale illustrates the mastery of navigating multiple publics, circumventing danger, and finding solace in Public Strangers.

According to Parker J. Palmer, "at bottom, the word 'public' means all of the people in a society, without distinction or qualification."[7] We encounter members of this broad populace on public streets and public transit, in city parks and at sidewalk cafes. In public life, strangers in pursuit of private interests meet each other and convey the subliminal messages that while we do not know each other, we occupy a common space.[8]

But public space and common ground are subjective realities. In the segregated South of my grandparents' childhood, certain public spaces were clearly demarcated "Whites Only." While the dividing lines of public terrain in the United States may not be as explicit as they once were, public demarcations to separate strangers still exist. The perceptive eye need not look hard to find public partitions in the form of redlining neighborhoods for tax purposes, community policing to target urban violence, and environmental hazards that toxify impoverished areas. Yet even with these dividing lines, in our daily round public worlds intersect, and strangers unexpectedly enter each other's lives.

Finding common ground in our private circles is often considered easier when we deal with those who are "like us." Individuals occupying our inner circle may share our race, sexual orientation, religious belief, or socioeconomic background. Yet the public is rife with difference that is capable of teaching us in wholly different ways than the comforts of our private spheres. In the company of Public Strangers, who exceed the bounds of our familiarity, we recognize both the potential for conflict and the power of human relatedness.

For Palmer, a healthy public life gives daily doses of potential conflict. When strangers meet and are forced to divvy up scarce resources, whether it be elbow room on a crowded subway or tax dollars for public schooling, conflict is inevitable. But public life teaches us that conflict is not always terminal. In both crowded spaces and difficult discourse we "learn to adjust, compromise, [and] correct our course so that conflict is minimized and the movement of the whole becomes possible."[9] In Fearless Dialogues we seek to create unique spaces where unlikely partners are challenged to make conscious adjustments to accommodate strangers and maneuver around potential conflict.

For instance, upon entering a Fearless Dialogue, everyone chooses a name tag from one of six categories: artist, healer, educator, neighbor, connector, or activist. Throughout our time together, persons in each category are strategically paired so that individuals who might not ordinarily speak to one another are placed on common ground. The felon and the judge, the millionaire and the unemployed, are challenged to draw upon their instinctive skills gained from public life to navigate conflict. In the best of circumstances, surprising connections between Public Strangers unfold. This truth strikes close to home for me.

My grandparents arrived as unemployed migrants in a midwestern factory town in the 1940s. They were strangers in a foreign land, with minimal education and a tenacious work ethic. Over time, Dub found work at a meatpacking plant, and he and Mary Jane scavenged scrap metal to make ends meet. A wizard with money, Granma learned how to make a dollar out of fifteen cents, and they built a five-bedroom home from the ground up for their growing family. This story sounds like the American folklore of pulling oneself up by one's bootstraps. While intestinal fortitude and unswerving faith in God are central to my forebears' narrative, it is also a story of human relatedness with Public Strangers.

Family sources tell me that Dub met a "good white man" who taught him how to read specific charts and grids so he could be hired at the meatpacking factory. Given his traumatic flight from segregated Mississippi, trusting a stranger, particularly a white man, seemed a risky proposition. Like my grandparents, who welcomed famished strangers for home-cooked meals, I learned (years later) that this "good white man" was also known for taking risks in the spirit of mutual aid. When stretched beyond the comfort of our private realm, our vantage of self-interest is altered. Freed from the restrictiveness of our private lives, in public we are apt to glimpse unexpected goodwill from unknown people. Such was the case for my grandfather on his job search in the heartland.

In a serendipitous twist to this American tale of Public Strangers, in 2013 I sat on a back porch in the Upper Midwest. I was invited into this home as a friend of a friend; in all accounts, I was a Public Stranger welcomed into a private circle. With hot tea in hand, the host asked a perfunctory question about my family history. I told the story of my grandparents' traumatic Mississippi exodus and their settlement in the Midwestern manufacturing town. The host raised his eyebrows, for he knew well of this same town. My kinfolk called the "good white man" Ol' Man Palmer. My host, Parker J. Palmer, knew him as his grandfather. Sometimes Public Strangers are more familiar than we think.

Placeholders for Public Strangers:
Transitional Objects for Transitional Spaces

"Greg, not so much salt. It'll give you high blood pressure. Not too much sugar, baby. You'll get diabetes. [Laugh.] If you drink too much water, you'll drown. Everything in moderation."

How I cherish the lessons learned at my grandmothers' welcome tables! Since their deaths, I better understand why many call southern cookin' "soul food." Long after the meals have digested, the food for thought still comforts the soul. On Saturdays, when I cook breakfast with my children and see the biscuits risin' in the oven, I hear Granma Simpson's voice. When I step outside and feel blanketed by the midnight pitch, I recall Grandma Ellison's lessons on country dark and taste homespun ice cream on the tip of my tongue. Oh, how I miss my grandmothers; but their soul food still nourishes me on my journey.

In addition to visiting me in my dreams, occasionally my grandmothers sit with me in public places. For example, some Sunday mornings, an old hymn will play in church. Before I catch myself, my eyes close and I'm rocking back and forth, taken by the tune. A tear falls and I recognize my grandmother "sitting with me." I wish I could open my eyes, and just one more time ask her for a peppermint tucked away in a ziploc bag at the bottom of her purse.

Not too long ago, one of my grandmothers sat with me in a meeting I had scheduled with a senior administrator at Emory. We had never spoken before, and because of the sensitive nature of our conversation, we met in her office. It was an unseasonably warm Atlanta day, but her workspace was frigid. When I entered the icebox, I noticed a basket of handmade quilts in the corner. To break the "proverbial ice" before our sensitive conversation, I inquired about the quilts. The administrator informed me that her retired grandmother, who lives in Mississippi, hand-stitched the quilts for her to give to office mates in their frozen tundra. "My Granma's from Mississippi, too. The quilts she made were so heavy, when you used them it felt like somebody was laying on you," I responded. Within seconds the tension around our forthcoming conversation dissipated, and this stranger and I became fast friends. Our grandmothers hovered above, but like magic carpets the quilts took us someplace else.

To explain the transcendent power of biscuit, blanket, and song, let us turn to the theories of D. W. Winnicott. Formally trained as a pediatrician before devoting his life to the study and practice of psychoanalysis, Winnicott spent a great deal of time observing babies and their mothers. From these observations, he gathered that the development of an infant's self is largely predicated on the presence of a "good-enough mother" who creates a secure base or holding environment. For Winnicott, a good-enough mother need not be perfect, clever, intellectually enlightened, or even the infant's biological mother. However, this parental presence must withdraw from her (or his) own needs and assume an "easy and unresented preoccupation" with the infant's care.[10] According to Winnicott, this unswerving devotion creates an illusion that the baby is the center of all things:

> If [the baby] is hungry and desires the breast [or bottle], it appears; he makes it appear; he creates the breast [or bottle]. If he is cold and starting to feel uncomfortable, it becomes warmer. He controls the temperature of the world around him; he creates his surroundings. The [good-enough mother] "*brings the world*" to the infant without delay, without skipping a beat.[11]

If the good-enough mother succeeds in responding to the infant's severe tests of hunger and trials of discomfort, these elements interact and produce an incubator for the child's self: a "holding environment." Winnicott's holding environment is "a physical and psychical space within which the infant is protected without knowing he is protected."[12] After this secure base is established and the good-enough mother gradually wanes in selfless preoccupation, the baby slowly recognizes his dependence. As a result of a safe and responsive holding environment, it dawns on the infant that she must now learn how to interact with the "not-me" world—the people and things in her surroundings—in order to survive and thrive.

Winnicott places primacy on the formative experiences in the infant-maternal relationship. In the earliest days of life, the good-enough mother selflessly devotes time and energy to creating a holding environment that responds to the infant's beck and call. When properly constituted, this holding environment creates the illusion that the child omnipotently controls the outside world and wields the power to demand food and dictate temperature change. However, as the good-enough mother's selfless devotion gradually wanes, the child slowly comes to realize that the "world does not revolve around me." This infantile epiphany is a developmental milestone for Winnicott, because the child is introduced to an objective reality that a world exists beyond oneself. While the subjective omnipotence created by the good-enough mother's holding remains a precious legacy and resource, the child must learn to engage the "not-me" world for survival.[13] Central to this phenomenon is the infant's adoption of a "not-me possession" that Winnicott calls a "transitional object."

Winnicott observes that days after birth, infants use fingers and thumbs to self-soothe. Months later, babies grow fond of stuffed animals, soft toys, and even blankets. For the pediatrician turned psychoanalyst, the child's attachment to these objects represents more than oral excitement and satisfaction. "Sooner or later in an infant's development there comes a tendency on the part of the infant to weave other-than-me objects into the personal pattern. To some extent these objects stand for the breast [or bottle]" and provide for the child a tangible sense of security and comfort reminiscent of the holding environment provided by the good-enough mother.[14]

As the child ages, the soft toy, corner of a blanket, word, mannerism, or tune becomes vitally important at the time of going to sleep, because it serves as a defense against anxiety and fear.[15] Winnicott further says that in some instances, the good-enough mother allows this precious object to get smelly and dirty because washing "it may introduce a break in continuity in the infant's experience, a break that may destroy the meaning and value of the object to the infant."[16] Furthermore, attachment to this transitional object that assuaged early feelings of anxiety, loneliness, and fear may persist well into childhood.

According to Winnicott, at some point in the child's development the physical object loses meaning but is not forgotten. Rather, it is internalized as a part of the child's inner reality. Once this transitional phenomenon is held within the growing child, memory of the once-cherished transitional object and the holding environment it symbolizes becomes a resource to fend off anxiety and fear.

Transitional phenomena internalized from our earliest holding environment can still secure us today. Rising biscuits on a Saturday can provide assurance that soul food will nourish generations to come. A Sunday hymn can summon the serenity of Granma's giving hands. Monday afternoon memories of grandmothers quilting can transform a tense conversation between strangers into fearless dialogue between fast friends. For these very reasons, Fearless Dialogues uses transitional objects as placeholders to extend Radical Hospitality to Public Strangers.

A placeholder is a word, symbol, or concept that occupies a position on behalf of something else. Like Winnicott's transitional objects, these placeholders serve as bridges between an individual's subjective experience and the objective reality of the outside world. Recognizing that anxieties and fears can run amok in the hearts and minds of Public Strangers, at Fearless Dialogues we utilize art, music, and food as placeholding transitional objects. While we cannot bring grandmothers and good-enough mothers into every room, we can utilize transitional objects that evoke memory and provide the feeling of a secure holding environment.

By design, when Fearless Dialogues hosts community conversations, we employ the services of local artisans. If food is to be served, a local cook or caterer is invited to prepare comfort foods for the gathering of unlikely partners. When the Public Strangers enter into the space, they hear all genres of music from hip-hop and jazz to classical and folk. These tunes are selected to tickle the ear and transition the anxious stranger to an environment that feels more homelike than novel. As the Public Strangers move toward their seats, artwork from around the world, picturing people of different ethnicities, genders, and backgrounds, lines the walls in an effort to send the subliminal message that all are welcome here. These intentionally set placeholders of food, music, and art serve as transitional objects capable of holding the environment for even Public Strangers to engage in dialogues fear lessly. These placeholders not only extend Radical Hospitality to Public Strangers; they also carve out space to behold the wisdom of Familiar Strangers.

FAMILIAR STRANGERS: MORE THAN MEETS THE EYE

Public Strangers need not be foreign. In fact, Familiar Strangers to whom we have never uttered a word oddly comfort us with their presence or alert us in their absence.

With some dread, I recall Emory's stadium-style lecture hall, which accommodated more than two hundred anxiety-ridden freshman chemistry students twice a week for a class designed to weed out freshmen who were less serious about the hard sciences. The college auditorium began to fill by 7:50 a.m. As on the New York City subway at rush hour, around five minutes to eight, throngs of students pressed through the double doors with unilateral focus: find a seat as fast as possible. Twice a week this was our daily commute.

My study partners and I sat on the third row from the front, always left of center. Even on the drowsiest of mornings, I took notice of the redheaded fella two rows ahead of me. Never did I introduce myself or bother to ask his name, but he was as much of a fixture in the stadium hall as the chalkboard and the professor. On the rare day that my redheaded colleague failed to fill his seat, I noticed. He was a Familiar Stranger. As I was a mainstay on row three and one of the few African American freshmen sitting front and center, it is likely that my colleagues (and the professor) who did not know my name also noticed *my* absences. We shared common space, but for all intents and purposes we were Familiar Strangers.

Almost a hundred years ago, native New Yorker and internationally renowned social psychologist Stanley Milgram published a brief essay titled "The Familiar Stranger: An Aspect of Urban Anonymity." Milgram examined New York City bystanders who witness criminal activity, but fail to offer aid,[17] intruders who upset the social system of waiting by cutting the line,[18] and even Familiar Strangers who share common space on subway platforms. According to Milgram and his laboratory mates, the Familiar Stranger "gains extreme familiarity with the faces of a number of persons, yet never interacts with them."[19] Like a developing friendship, the frozen relationship of Familiar Strangers is a process that takes time. To become a Familiar Stranger "a person (1) has to be observed, (2) repeatedly for a certain time period, and (3) without any interaction." As time elapses, barriers arise between Familiar Strangers, chances of salutatory pleasantries diminish, and recognizable faces blend into the environment as part of the urban scenery.[20]

Milgram and his colleagues conducted a social experiment by photographing morning commuters on a New York City subway platform. The images pictured clusters of commuters standing back to back or facing straight ahead, all close in proximity, but emotionally distant and removed. The following week, the researchers distributed the photographs to the morning passengers with a cover letter about their study and a questionnaire about the phenomenon of Familiar Strangers. The findings were amazing! Nearly 90 percent of those questioned were familiar with at least one platform stranger. The average commuter recognized at least four persons with whom they had never shared a word.[21]

In addition to the study's statistics, the feedback uncovered that many passengers often think of their fellow commuters, imagining what kind of lives they lead and jobs they hold. Milgram surmised that Familiar Strangers shared an unspoken bond to mutually ignore each other without any implication of hostility. However, under critical circumstances, Familiar Strangers would mobilize to speak to, stand alongside, and support each other, despite the prior pact of silence. These findings provide a key opening for Fearless Dialogues to create spaces for unlikely partners who rarely interact to have transformative encounters that alter the lives of self and other.[22]

Beholding Familiar Strangers:
Granmas, Greyhounds, and Guns

Funny story. Not long after we were married, Antoinette and I visited Granma Simpson one evening. Recently widowed and living in a large house, she slept with a loaded pistol. So when she invited us to sit with her in the bedroom, Granma moved her firearm to the nightstand before motioning for us to sit on the bed. Noticing that my wife was visibly alarmed, my pistol-packing Granma turned to Antoinette and said, "I protect my own." Then she shared this unforgettable story.

Granma hated airplanes. She only voyaged where her two feet could carry her or the spinning wheels of a car, bus, or train traveled. That evening she told us of one excursion to visit a family relative. On this particular bus trip, she journeyed alone, but her Greyhound[23] was delayed. For hours, she waited in a seedy bus station. To pass the time, she reverted to her custom of scanning the space, imagining the life stories of the people around her, and praying for the strangers on their journeys. After surveying the room, she locked eyes with an unnerved single mother traveling with her young children. As a mother of eleven, Granma knew all too well the struggles of antsy children on long trips. For her the story of this overwhelmed mother was more familiar than strange. While the overwrought mother sought to ease her anxious children, Granma noticed a suspicious man lurking and eyeing the distracted mother's handbag.

In a slow gaunt, Granma gathered her belongings and strolled over to the overstimulated mother. In minutes, they struck up a conversation about parenting and travels, yet Granma's eyes still scanned the room. Like a predator stalking his prey, a mysterious man lurching around moved in to strike on the overwrought mother and the sweet ol' woman. Growing up in Mississippi, Granma disliked huntin', but she knew her way around the wild. So she stuck a hand in her purse and looked the lurch in the eye. With her trigger finger on the concealed weapon, she said to the lurch, "If you know what's best, you should walk away . . ." As the point of the story, Granma smiled at us, leaned over to Antoinette, and chuckled, "I protect my own."

In a seedy bus station full of strangers, Granma scanned the room and took particular notice of an overextended mother and her children. Granma knew the struggles of overextension all too well; this mother's story was a familiar one that hit close to home. In the process of connecting eyes and beholding each other, a silent and sacred bond was formed between two mothers. The strength of this bond quickened in crisis as Granma noticed the malevolent intentions of the lurch. Granma felt beholden to the mother and her children, even though minutes earlier they had yet to exchange a single word. For over a decade, I have been fascinated by Granma's quickened bond, social responsibility, and Radical Hospitality to this woman she had never met. To better understand this exchange, let us return to Stanley Milgram's work on how Familiar Strangers study each other closely and form unique and unspoken bonds of kinship.

Recall Milgram's findings revealed that while commuters had an unvoiced pact to silently interact on the subway platform, they took notice when a fellow passenger did not show up for their morning commute. Milgram's research-based insights add that Familiar Strangers also wondered about the jobs and lives of their platform peers and, in certain circumstances, were motivated to speak to, stand alongside, or support them. Consider this example that Milgram offers:

> A woman collapsed on the streets of Brooklyn, not far from her apartment house. She had been a Familiar Stranger to another resident of the street for years. The resident immediately took responsibility for the unconscious woman, not only calling an ambulance, but riding with her to the hospital to make certain she was treated properly, and to assure that her possessions were not stolen by the ambulance attendants. She said later that she had felt a special responsibility for the woman, because they had seen each other for years, even if they had never spoken.[24]

Milgram's studies suggest that Familiar Strangers possess the capacity to behold each other and, in rare circumstances, can become beholden to their neighbors. Word play is necessary for further explanation.

The earliest accounts of the word "behold" refer to "regarding or contemplating with the eye." Such seeing is not circumstantial, because beholding "requires an active voluntary exercise of the faculty of vision." Given this definition, Milgram's research implies Familiar Strangers do not simply place their platform peers or nearby neighbors in their line of sight each day. Rather, the Familiar Strangers actually become visible to one another. As beholders, commuters not only see with their eyes; they also contemplate with them, creating story lines about jobs, schedules, and lives.

At Fearless Dialogues we take great effort to encourage unlikely partners to behold Familiar Strangers who gather for conversation. The process of beholding is first modeled by the host, with the animators' eye contact and initial greeting, "It's good to see you." To prepare unlikely partners for eye-to-eye conversations with other community thought leaders, the Familiar Strangers are welcomed into the Living Museum. There they find animators standing on chairs and holding provocative images at guests' eye level. Face to face with captivating photos and works of art, the Familiar Strangers are challenged to contemplate with their eyes: "When you look at this photo, who do you see? Who does this person symbolize in your life? Is it someone from your family, your job, your hometown?" Customarily, the contemplating eyes of Familiar Strangers drift upward as they search the annals of their mind for a familiar face, a familiar story. These modules prepare a beholder's contemplative eyes to see the gifts in the Familiar Strangers with whom they will soon be in conversation.

Milgram's research suggests that as time elapses, Familiar Strangers do more than behold with the eye; they silently become beholden to others. According to the *Oxford English Dictionary*, the word "beholden" denotes an attachment or moral obligation to a person. Milgram's example of the Brooklyn neighbors attests to the unique shared bond of Familiar Strangers when it is fostered by prolonged observation.

At Fearless Dialogues conversations, we rarely have the opportunity to foster bonds between Familiar Strangers through prolonged observation. For this reason, in the Laboratory of Discovery we

1. practice Radical Hospitality to lessen anxiety and reduce power differences;
2. employ artistic mediums as transitional objects to reframe sterile and hostile environments into spaces for lively and engaging interaction; and
3. utilize research-based experiments to enhance vulnerable truth sharing and to foster connections.

While we have yet to learn of a Fearless Dialogues partner leaping into an ambulance to accompany a neighbor they know only in passing, we can attest to hugs shared between rival gang members, healing tears between estranged coworkers, and twisted smiles of awe and responsibility as neighbors stretch out their three-feet measuring tape and feel beholden to each other.

INTIMATE STRANGERS: FLATLINES, FAULTLINES, AND THE STRANGE FREEDOM OF CRISIS

Intimate Strangers share more than common space. With risk and gall, they extend themselves for the common good. Some, like the Good Samaritan of old, are lauded for their heroism. Others make a living by lifting the spirits of sojourners wandering in the strange lands of crisis. As my father and I learned on one particularly traumatic journey, a common bond with a complete stranger can buoy life even when we are surrounded by death.

Startled from my uneasy sleep, I heard a man moaning. "Code Blue" bawled from the loudspeaker, nurses and doctors started running, and the wheels of the inclined bed spun loudly as they rushed down the hospital's hallway. In seconds I returned to consciousness and glanced over my shoulder from my faux-leather recliner. The IV dripped, the machines beeped, and the tubing coiled in and out of my father's body. The antiseptic cleanliness of his hospital room tickled my nostrils, and I grappled with the strangeness of crisis, the anxiety of the space.

Amid the commotion beyond the door, Lakisha entered in her navy scrubs and brand new sneakers. "Mr. Ellison, I'm here to check your vitals." Her face was unfamiliar, yet her steadied voice invited calm. After scanning his barcoded wristband and inquiring about his name and date of birth, she spoke to Greg Sr. as more than a patient, to me as more than a concerned observer. While checking his temperature and tinkering with the beeping apparatus, she cracked tasteful jokes. In between laughs, Dad disclosed with uncustomary ease vulnerabilities about his current condition. With all that was happening in the wee hours across the hospital wing, we glimpsed home. Greeted by the strangeness of crisis, in a strange foreboding place, nurse Lakisha welcomed us as an Intimate Stranger.

Intimate Stranger. A paradoxical word pair, indeed. How might one be closely acquainted and wholly unfamiliar simultaneously? Years before assuming his professorship at Princeton Theological Seminary and advising my dissertation, Robert C. Dykstra was forced to reckon with this contradiction of terms. As an emergency room chaplain for the medical center in Princeton, young Dykstra found himself standing alongside families in strange and uncertain crises. Oftentimes, finitude and flatlines lingered in the conscious mind of visitors awaiting news of the condition of their loved ones. While favorable news garnered sighs of relief for some, others belched out guttural moans when the strangeness of death and loss entered their life.

Week after week Dykstra encountered death in the presence of teary-eyed patients and hospital visitors. There were tragic deaths by accidental hanging, car crashes, or stab wounds and more expected passings of the elderly by cardiac arrest or other traumas.[25] Regardless of the state of demise, loved ones felt the sting. Even in times when death does not have the final say, survival can bring loss in the form of life-altering infirmity. Yet even in the presence of loss and the company of tears, the flatline-lingering, life-altering waiting room doubled as a sanctuary for the young chaplain with eyes to see and ears to hear.

In the sanctuary of crisis and the company of strangers, a strange freedom abides.

Dykstra came to this revelation in a moment when caring with a woman whose twenty-six-year-old daughter had just died by suicide. While Dykstra was talking with the bereaved mother, she began shouting at him, "I hate God! I hate God! I hate him! I hate him!"[26] A few minutes later, her parish priest arrived in the waiting room. As she sat before the priest, the mother's demeanor shifted. She was not only cordial and composed; she also humbly expressed her gratitude for the priest's presence. Just as my father found uncustomary ease in full disclosure with nurse Lakisha, this mother stepped over the fault lines of decorum and unabashedly disclosed her repressed truth to a chaplain she had never met and might never see again. In both situations "the suffering person [felt the] freedom to say or do whatever he or she needed to, knowing that because the [caregiver was] a stranger, the victim need not be held accountable for it."[27] The intensity of crisis, coupled with the unfamiliarity of a benevolent other, creates ideal conditions for the strange freedom of truth telling.

Holding Intimate Strangers in the Crucible of Crisis:
Bringing the World to the Parking Lot

I thought I knew my father well. After all, we had shared the same name for more than twenty-two years. He cooked me oatmeal and over-darkened toast to "coat my stomach" on wintry days in grade school. Through our teenage years, he toted my brother and me to our basketball games and gave us the evil eye when we jittered in Sunday morning worship. For many of my boyhood years, after church Greg Sr., the accountant, set up a card table in front of the television in the den. In this makeshift office, twenty pounds of tax documents and a plug-in calculator (the size of a small laptop, today) sat atop the card table with pencil-thin legs. With his left hand, Dad rifled through legal pads filled with numbers while the fingers on his right glided over numbered keys as if his calculator was a baby grand piano. As the sportscaster commentated from the television, the pencil-thin table legs swayed side to side, and the calculator churned out its tune. The entire family knew not to disturb this weekly ritual. Back then, Dad wasn't much on words or public displays of affection. He worked hard, cared for his family, and went to church. In my mind, he was content with his Sunday solitude and the "big piece of chicken" at dinner.[28] But in March 1999, I learned that I barely knew the man whose name I inherited.

The call came around 10 a.m. As a senior in college, I was just knocking the crust from my eyes and preparing for an afternoon class. The voice on the other end of the phone unnerved me. I immediately dropped the phone and rushed to northwest Atlanta to pick up my younger brother from the high school I had graduated from just four years prior. So taken by the news I shared, the principal, who knew our family well, jumped in his car and trailed me and my brother to the meeting place.

Around six thirty that morning, my father was kidnapped at gunpoint. Like every other day, with coffee in tow, he walked down the paved entryway to open the office. As he rifled for his keys, an armed assailant approached him and jabbed a pistol in his back. He took the keys, marched my father back to the car, forced him in the trunk, and drove off. In the darkness of that cramped space, my father talked to his abductor. From the trunk, he prayed for him aloud. Hours later, the car stopped and the blinding light of day startled my father as the trunk flung open. "Drive to the nearest bank." Careful not to turn to his right and glimpse the abductor's face, my father drove to his local credit union. Fully reclined in the passenger's seat, the gunman pushed his weapon in my father's side. After withdrawing several hundred dollars, my father pulled away from the bank and the gunman leapt out of the moving car. At 10 a.m. I received the call from my father's secretary. "Your father was kidnapped this morning. . . . I need you to meet him at your church."

Shortly before 11:00 a.m., my brother, the principal, and I pulled into the church parking lot. My mother and pastor stood outside of the front door of the church anticipating our arrival. In the parking lot, open arms received our confounded minds and our troubled hearts. Tears replaced words. Then a prayer raised to the heavens. On the blacktop of the cathedral on Cascade, we held each other, recognizing that life as we knew it would forever change.

Minutes later, my father turned into the lot. Little did we know that moments earlier the same car he drove had doubled as a darkened cell. He stopped the vehicle well before the entrance of the church and shakily removed his 6-foot-3-inch frame from behind the wheel. With tears streaming down his face, he ran toward us. We sprinted to him. Steps away from the Lord's house, we held each other. In the company of the principal and the pastor, my father kissed my mother, my brother, and me. With a crucible of truth that only crisis can uncover, he fearlessly said, "I love you so much."

Could this be my father? His emotions and vulnerability made him unrecognizable. In a bold display of public affection, father, mother, and sons stood teary-eyed in the parking lot as Intimate Strangers. On the white-lined asphalt, a holding environment was created to contain the raw, unfiltered emotions of deep-seated pain and wordless joy.

For nearly twenty years, I have reflected on crucibles fashioned by nurses in hospital rooms, chaplains in ER waiting rooms, pastors and principals in parking lots, and others capable of holding the truth shared between Intimate Strangers. These ruminations have framed how Fearless Dialogues crafts a container to hold the untapped gifts and undiscovered stories of strangers encountering each other in the seat of crisis.

We now take a closer look at the evolution of the word "crucible" and how a crucible might serve as a unique "holding environment" for Intimate Strangers to unearth new understandings of self and other. According to the *Oxford English Dictionary*, the word "crucible" was first used in 1475, in reference to "a vessel, usually of earthenware, made to endure great heat, used for fusing metals." As time evolved, the definition of crucible as a literal melting pot took on figurative forms. Two such iterations of the word refer to "crucible" as "a place of severe test or trial" and "a situation in which different elements interact to produce something new." In order to welcome Intimate Strangers who approach hard conversations under the duress of severe trials and tests, Fearless Dialogues must create a vessel that can endure great stress and allow different personalities to interact to produce something new. This crucible for Intimate Strangers is called a "holding environment," Winnicott's psychoanalytic term introduced earlier.

Winnicott views the infant-maternal relationship as a metaphor to examine how individuals respond in care settings and interact with the world. In his work as a psychoanalyst, Winnicott sought to create a holding environment for his patients, much like the one created by the good-enough mother "who brings the world" to the infant to foster a physically and psychically secure base. In his essay titled "Cure," Winnicott aptly referred to a psychoanalyst as a "host" who is not concerned solely with "interpreting the repressed unconscious [but] . . . the provision of a professional setting for trust, in which such work may take place."[29] Two hosts, doubling as good-enough mothers, took the responsibility of holding my family in the crucible of crisis.

On that spring morning in 1999, my father's abduction shook our family at the core. We were strangers to crisis, and in our immense anxiety unrecognizable elements of our personalities emerged. Yes, we intimately knew each other as relatives. But prior to that morning only once had I seen my father cry. Public displays of affection escaped my memory. For the first time in my life, the man I perceived as superhuman and the pinnacle of strength appeared mortal and frail. Yet our family received the care of two good-enough mothers in the form of principal and pastor "fathers."

Far from a hospital chaplain and more like a stern disciplinarian, Dr. Samuel L. Hill, the principal at Frederick Douglass High School, gave my brother and me space to share our deepest fears and pains in his office. Even though it was during the school day, Dr. Hill preoccupied himself with our extraordinary predicament and followed us to the church. Once in the church parking lot, about twenty feet from the door, stood my mother and the Rev. Walter L. Kimbrough. Recognizing the magnitude of the trauma, Rev. Kimbrough did not require us to walk beyond our car door to receive a caring embrace. He "brought the world" to us. Like the care we received in Principal Hill's office, our pastor's care forged another vessel to purge our pain, contain our fears.

Before my father's car broke the horizon, we stood hand in hand on the white-lined black asphalt and prayed for his health and sanity, and for our strength and humility. By the time my father drove into the lot, a holding environment had already been created to contain his severe tests and our traumatic trial. That day the parking lot doubled as a crucible. In it, the undiscovered emotions of Intimate Strangers interacted and produced a new and deeper love for family members whom we thought we had known already.

At Fearless Dialogues, we seek to fashion a holding environment that can contain all manner of crises. Under Winnicott's tutelage, we believe that as animators we bear the responsibility of withdrawing from our own needs and assuming an "easy and unresented preoccupation" with the unlikely partners soon to gather. Learning from good-enough "mothers" like Dr. Hill, we seek to create a physical and psychic space where unlikely partners feel protected enough to share their fears. Simultaneously, we fully understand that trust does not come with ease. For this reason, we internalize the wisdom of good-enough mother Kimbrough, and we pray for unlikely partners weeks, sometimes even months, before their feet begin moving toward conversation. Finally, on that prayerfully anticipated day, just as the Intimate Strangers "open their car doors," we bring the world to them. Through Radical Hospitality, we assure them time and time again that we have been expecting their arrival and they are most welcome in the sacred space to share their gifts. These deliberate and prayerful actions create a crucible-like holding environment for Intimate Strangers to interact.

As a Fearless Dialogues animator, at times I play the role of Intimate Stranger. It is a blessing to create secure spaces for unlikely partners to engage deeply. However, as animator, I also bear the unique burden of shouldering unfiltered truths and seeing persons in trauma. Looking back on his role as a chaplain and Intimate Stranger, Dykstra articulates this burden by reflecting on the risk and the reward of being fully present with persons in some of the most critical moments of their lives.[30] Dykstra discloses that accompanying persons through the gauntlet of trauma created in him an "escalating sense of utter helplessness and inadequacy."[31] In providing space for suffering persons to bear their wounds, as a chaplain and caregiver he was bruised and scarred. In order not to become calloused to death and cold to loss, caregivers and hosts must contend with their own mortality, the frailty of heartache, and the antinomy of why bad things happen to good people. "In coming as a stranger to strangers in a situation of strangeness," even the good-hearted Samaritan must reckon with the strangers within.[32]

THE STRANGER WITHIN: TOURISTS
OF THE INNER LANDSCAPE

There are strangers among us. Sadly, too many lie within. The city streets of our hearts bustle with endless foot traffic. Like Times Square, Trafalgar Square, and Tiananmen Square layered one atop the other, the world of the heart attracts untold tourists. These curious out-of-towners explore our inner landscape, posing before the monumental moments we hold most dear. We overhear their unknown tongues rumbling up from the deep or perhaps even shift our gaze to the visitors' direction. But as phantoms their faces remain shadow-cast; a closer look reveals a throng of strangers standing suspiciously in darkness. Huddled around the id, they inflict terror and instill fright. We know not whence they came. Yet we feel their shadowed presence when we take a new job, strike out to foreign lands, or enter a crowded room of unfamiliar faces. If these feelings are left unchecked, when we move into uncharted regions, we may project our fears of the shadowed tourists onto the living faces before us. Therefore, we must befriend the strangers within, lest the unexamined and unchecked traffic of the heart breed anxiety toward the stranger and bleed hostility toward our neighbor.

Not that long ago, a series of unforeseen events triggered a fit of rage in me that halted my ability to write. Having counseled young men exiting the prison system, I had seen rage on the visage of others many, many times. In their presence, I heard rage in trembled voices and felt it hovering like a toxic smog. But in my mind, I was different. Then Rage reared his head during a lunch meeting with a companion I had just met. To my knowledge, this companion intended me no harm; we had spoken for only a matter of moments. Yet an unfamiliar feeling boiled in me. A whisper rumbled from the depths: "Reach across the table and break his jaw!" Though I had not thrown a punch since fourth grade, it took every iota of energy in my thirty-four-year-old self not to clinch my fist and swing. Never before had I recognized Rage's habitation in my heart. But on that day I learned he was there to stay and had been awaiting my visit.

On a February morning in 2011, I stood before the mirror and met Rage. He looked me squarely in the eye. To the casual observer, we'd look like twins, but his likeness seemed misshapen—fractured, if you will. As I turned in disgust from the reflection before me, Rage whispered, "I'm leasing a flat down below. Come see me, won't you?"

For weeks, I tried to ignore his simmer, his sting. But in occasional conversations, sly and sarcastic comments surfaced from the deep and sauntered from my lips. Standing witness to the shock on my conversation partners' faces, I could feel Rage's chuckle. "Come see me . . . ," he'd whisper. But I'd snuff out his voice. As weeks turned to months, at home I began to notice that my verbal utterances were several decibels above normal. In my high-volume rants, my loved ones looked on in disbelief. In the silent aftermath, with head bowed in shame I questioned, "Who am I? What have I become?" The stranger in me had become a foe, while I was an ally in his spoils.

On a November evening of that same year, I stood again transfixed before the mirror. Rage's face had become my own. In fright and disbelief, I mustered courage for the inward journey. I visited Rage in his flat below.

> i know this hood
> so i checked it out
> i park my thoughts
> approach the house
> "greg, you've seen this guy before . . .
> own your shit knock on his door"
> see through the portal feel his soul
> he sees me too
> through the small peephole
> he knows my fossils and my name
> my goals, intentions
> this ain't a game
>
> gateway open
>
> i stare him down!
>
> Rage slams the door
> i kick it in, but just before
> i step in and examine his house
> i calm my nerves
> internal flames to douse

on one hand i feel so far from home
on the other i'm not alone
the bolt turns
that sucker locked me in
now i'm imprisoned from within

on a centered table light radiates
and now I feel so far from hate
his home is my home
purity, there
rage untainted is full of care
no varnish to cover blemished wood
remind me life's cracks are fully good
Rage no longer stranger, but friend
His creative fire now burns within.

In the poem above, I personified the strange emotion, Rage. For months, he not only tormented my inner life; he also created friction in family settings and fissures in daily conversation. As these rifts became too much to bear, I reconciled that no longer would I live a divided life. The stranger *in* me is *of* me. To ignore and split apart this emotion that is woven into the fabric of my being is to be untrue to my self. Thus, in order to speak with full integrity, to write with bold authenticity, and to exist in the world undivided, I had to meet and make peace with my nemesis.

To face this stranger required me to acknowledge that little difference lay between me and the young men I counseled. Standing before the mirror, I recounted their confessions of rape, murder, and malignancy. How difficult it was to realize that even with my firmly rooted faith and measured moral compass, what lay in them was resident in me. Theory and practice taught me to introduce them to their rage, so that it would not rule them unawares. Even though I had glimpsed Rage's face in me, it took nine months to practice what I preached. On that November evening, I stood in the flat of my soul. In the home that Rage had built, I came to understand that this stranger in me was puppeting my interactions with the outside world. Locked in the empty box where Rage once lived, he and I became one. I found a space of welcome where the once-shadowed visitor became a friend in me and a friend to me.

In time, I noticed my disposition change. Probing conversations and hearty dialogue replaced the shortened comments and the curt sarcasm that had rolled off my tongue so effortlessly months before. The volume knob on my voice box turned down, and sanctity returned to my home. Finally, the flood gates opened, and words upon words flowed freely from my soul down to my fingertips and onto the screen. Welcoming the Stranger Within actually welcomes our true self home.

Have you welcomed the Stranger Within into your home? If not, how is the lack of your relationship with the shadowed stranger impacting your interaction with the world? How difficult it is to greet fellow sojourners we have never seen, if we are fearful of the stranger we met in the mirror many, many years ago. In order to create a free and open space for the strangers among us, we must first be radically hospitable to the self.

Moving the Host to Welcome the Stranger Within

In order to receive a guest, the host must create a free and open space within. However, hospitably emptying one's self to welcome the fullness of another is much easier said than done. Our minds "seethe with endless traffic, with noisy rumblings."[33] Worries and concerns over unresolved questions and open-ended situations preoccupy our inner world. Fears of change pepper our inner landscape such that a bad certainty far outweighs a promising risk. Crucial deadlines, bill payments, and time-sensitive e-mails populate our inner life. Our inner terrain becomes so jam-packed with ideas, opinions, judgments, and fears that little acreage remains for self-reflection, discovery, or the warm welcome of others.[34]

Even though the traffic of the daily round creates gridlock in our minds, there still exists unclaimed acreage in the soul. To greet the Stranger Within and be readied to welcome and accept others, we must *move away from* the internal congestion of the mind and *move toward* the open space of the soul. How is this done, you ask? Let's seek the wisdom of famed American psychologist Carl Rogers.

Lauded for ages because of his uncanny ability to create safe, warm, and empathetic therapeutic environments, Rogers proved skillful in aiding his clients to move toward the open space of the heart. In his essay "To Be That Self Which One Truly Is," Rogers plots the direction taken by some of his clients seeking to discern their aim in life.[35] While he does not reveal the length of time that he sojourns with these clients, he does accentuate the importance of their gradual movement *away from* the traffic and *toward* the open space where the undiscovered self resides.

Moving Away From . . .

Some of us are caught in a facade. Rogers describes a teenage male expressing deep fear of being exposed by peers as something he is not. The young man equally resists disclosing to Rogers who he thinks he really is. Like Rogers's client, I hid behind a facade and denied the possibility that Rage could take root in me. I, too, sought to distance myself from this volatile emotion that I saw in the eyes of incarcerated young men. At times the facade faltered, and I feared exposure. Both the teenage client and I sought to move away fearfully from a self we were convinced that we were not. However, "in doing so we were beginning to define, albeit negatively, who we were."[36] For Rogers, recognizing and moving away from facades marks a milestone in becoming a person who welcomes the Stranger Within.

Rogers also deemed it necessary to move away from "oughts."[37] Like a legion of voices constantly whispering in our ears, imperatives of who we "ought to be" filter into our consciousness, occupy our mind, and pattern our thinking and daily practice. These internal voices originate from family, culture, faith commitments, and professional expectations; left unchecked, these influencers may distance us from the open space of the heart. In my situation, I could not grapple with the reality that though I was a pastor, counselor, and Ivy-League-trained professor, this Rage simmered in me. Given my upbringing and training, I thought that I "ought to be" able to snuff out such a temperamental emotion. Not the case. Like Rogers's clients, I had to move away from oughts and own the fact that "what is most repulsive in others mirrors some fragment in me."[38]

Moving away from facades and oughts draws one nearer to the repressions in the self.[39] Off the beaten path of conscious thinking, repressed emotions, like strangers in the midst, await engagement. Once conscious of these inner strangers, in order "to be the self which one truly is," we must move toward them.

Moving Toward . . .

One of Rogers's adult male clients felt an unsettling disdain whenever he experienced childish feelings. In one session the small-boy aspect of himself emerged, and with shock the client exclaimed, "That's an emotion I've never felt clearly—one that I've never been/seen."[40] Rogers explains that after this alarming encounter, over time this client began to accept and embrace his younger self as part of himself. With a growing sense of acceptance and embrace, the client learned to live closer to his feelings and welcome the small-boy aspect of himself. Rogers highlights that by moving toward and living into an open, friendly, close relationship to our own experience, we unleash the possibility of having community within.[41]

On that November evening years ago, I stood transfixed before the mirror, seeking the community and companionship of Rage. Having long perceived Rage as a frightening enemy, I faced myself and finally felt the emotion clearly. In Rage's presence, I felt the tensions of explosive flame and creative fire. That encounter with Rage was a new undertaking; prior to that moment, I would not permit myself to experience Rage, because of fear. To my surprise, what I found in me was far less terrible than imagined. Like Rogers's clients, when I moved toward living in an open, friendly, close relationship with my own experience, I gradually began to recognize Rage as a friendly resource and not as a foreboding stranger.[42]

With the companionship of the Stranger Within turned friend, the once small, unclaimed acreage of my inner terrain widened. Less fearful of what I might uncover, I found that sources of information and relationships with others I had once closed off miraculously opened. This experience perfectly aligns with Rogers's theory. He explains that moving toward a greater openness within leads the undivided self toward greater acceptance of others and a heightened ability to value and appreciate both one's own experience and that of others.[43]

The movement away from facades and oughts and toward openness of experience and acceptance of others is the consummate journey of the Fearless Dialogues animator. The host committed to the journey of moving away from oughts and moving toward self-acceptance comes to understand that Radical Hospitality is not about "changing other people by our convictions, stories, advice and proposals."[44] To the contrary, the host, who is on her own journey, knows the inherent power of laying aside one's preoccupations. In the free and open space of Radical Hospitality and Fearless Dialogue, both host and stranger are given license to simply "be that self which one truly is."

A FINAL WORD
THE WELCOME TABLE: A RETROSPECTIVE

As a young boy with Simpson blood, I ate for sport in all locales. To my delight, our church family greeted the sacred meal of Holy Communion with the same reverence that Granma had when feeding throngs of kinfolk. Indeed, First Sundays were earmarked as ritualized services of remembrance, punctuated by celebrating the Eucharist. But that's not all. At the start of every month, this high holy day showcased the whole community, and Radical Hospitality shone through the sanctuary in both word and deed.

With our red-paged Methodist hymnal in hand, Pastor Lowery invited all those who were able to stand to follow the printed liturgy and to read the boldfaced words. Each spoken word bound the congregation together and drew us nearer to the blessed elements. Just before family after family would leave their burgundy-cushioned pews to partake of the holy elements, we read an age-old prayer in unison: "We do not presume to come to this thy *Table*, O merciful Lord, trusting in our own righteousness, but in thy manifold and great mercies. We are not worthy so much as to gather up the crumbs under thy *Table*. But thou art the same Lord . . ."

Our table was an off-white altar rail at the front of the church. It stood in contrast to the maroon carpet like the sliver of cream-cheese frosting on a three-layered red velvet cake. Though thin in frame, this altar served the same purpose as the wide statuesque table at Granma's. This was an open table, and all were welcomed to partake of its goodness. And if Pastor Lowery's invitation did not underscore this salutation, our singing did. Without fail, on every First Sunday we sang the refrain of the most memorable church tune of my youth: "I'm gonna sit at the welcome table. I'm gonna sit at the welcome table one of these days, Hallelujah!"[45]

As these rhythmic words of Radical Hospitality filled the sanctuary, all would make their way up to the sumptuous-looking altar. Swaying from side to side in flowing purple and white robes, Ms. Sally led the choir from the loft. Row after row they received the bread and drank the wine. Standing shoulder to shoulder with Rev. Lowery, the elder mothers, beaming in Clorox-white suits, ensured no empty cup remained on the table after the diners feasted; so too every basket of wafers remained full. Hallelujah! After the robed chorale, the male usher board in their black ties methodically welcomed congregants in pew after pew—from the last row in the balcony to the first row in the church—to join our pastor and the elder mothers at the off-white altar in front. As we lined the outer walls of the sanctuary awaiting the symbolic feast, toddlers tugged on their fathers' trousers, teenagers stood close to Mom, old men shifted their weight on to wooden canes, and saints resembling Granma adjusted their big church hats. As our inner-city church was minutes away from four universities, it was no surprise to see collegians line the wall. Even more memorable were the times when members of Atlanta's homeless community stood patiently alongside the middle-class family clad in their Sunday best. After the walls were cleared, Rev. Lowery invited the ushers to the table. In gratitude for their service as hosts, he affectionately called them "doorkeepers in the house of the Lord." However, this high holy moment of hospitality did not close until the ministers had eaten and the elders and infirm who could not walk to the altar were served the elements in their seats.

Every First Sunday, I saw a welcome table. All were family. None were strangers. We were moved, held, beholden to each other, and transitioned to a place of serenity and love. We were earthly bound, but Radical Hospitality made the sanctuary heaven-like. While there is rarely a physical altar in Fearless Dialogues conversations, we seek to infuse spaces with a warm and inviting spirit where neighbors can feast on the wisdom of neighbors and broken communities can find kinship in the company of strangers.

4

When Pupils See

Beyond the Fear of Plopping

The cutting silence left a crimson stain on the classroom floor. On day one, this wound opened. For the next five years, I'd fight to stay alive.

Twenty minutes before the inflicted pain, I descended the steps of Princeton Seminary's chapel to take my place in a most unusual basement classroom. The old stone walls of the chapel's cellar sound-proofed the room so that even the slightest sigh bounced around in search of readied ears. But my colleagues and the professor seemed unfazed by the room's acoustics when my first doctoral seminar began.

For the opening fifteen minutes of class, senior colleagues and the professor tossed around jargon-heavy words like cotton balls. But I had done my homework prior to this initial seminar, so I entered the back-and-forth exchange of ideas. Within seconds of tossing out my first words, I recognized the faces around the table going blank. The hairs on my arm stood on end, and the subterranean room felt chilly, hollow, cavernous. I continued to speak and could hear my own words muffling in my ears. Like a plunger muting a trumpet, my noteworthy notions bounced off the walls and crashed to the floor.

When my brief soliloquy ended, the faces around the table re-turned to a state of liveliness, and the conversation continued as if I had not uttered a single word. A few minutes later, a senior colleague was complimented for his genius after echoing the words I had just . . . previously . . . stated. At that moment, I took notice of the blood on the floor, but I could not fathom how deeply I'd been cut.

Semester after semester, microaggressions mounted, ate away at my hope, and left the unsightly psychic wound raw and unscabbed. "You write about too much Black stuff, Greg," one said. "Focus more on the theory, and less on communal practices," one instructed. "Creativity is your greatest strength and your greatest weakness. Just follow the instructions and do the assignment," advised another. Each seemingly well-intentioned voice stuck a salted finger in my open wound. Hemorrhaging from the identity assaults, day after day I halfheartedly hobbled in and out of classrooms.

Having seen "real" plight, I sealed my lips and likened my doctoral dilemmas to "problems of the privileged." I suffered in silence. Unacknowledged, unsupported, and unscabbed, I heard the death toll of hopelessness begin to ring. But my pride would not allow the world to see my inner toil, so "I wore a mask that grins and lies, to hide my cheeks and shade my eyes."[1] For months on end, I laughed at humorless jokes and nodded my head even when I did not agree. With each disingenuous performance, the mask melded to my face, fused to my identity. After this eighteen-month charade, I not only felt unacknowledged on campus; I found myself unrecognizable in the mirror. Through masking, I deepened the wound, as I became invisible to others and to myself. (. . . sigh . . .)

By month nineteen, I had reached a breaking point, a turning point—a crossroads, if you will. "Shall I descend deeper into the shadows, or shall I spotlight the invisible?" In choosing the latter, I sought to understand my lot and research the life and livelihood of others who felt unacknowledged, unseen, and unheard. In the life and work of Ralph Ellison and Howard Washington Thurman I found clarity. William James, Alice Miller, and W. E. B. Du Bois offered theoretical structures to frame my theory around muteness and invisibility. Beckoning to me from the printed page, these voices spurred my hope and salved my wound. But blood still trickled forth. Suturing my psychic sore required a community of reliable others far beyond Princeton's Ivy-green.

In the sleepy town of Somerset, I pried off the mask on my counselor's couch. On other days, I traveled further north and just minutes from Montclair's main drag, I rediscovered black excellence over catfish dinners at my godmother's kitchen table. The gracious members of Newark's Memorial West Presbyterian nurtured my fragile voice back to health; before long I stood behind that rickety old lectern and preached sermons with creative boldness. Miles from that chapel classroom, as I sat on a couch, stood in a pulpit, and swapped stories over plates of fried fish, I learned to laugh again, to communicate authentically. With my hope healing in this community of reliable others, the open wound began to close, and life returned to my limbs. Then, I received a call from Uth Turn . . .

This chapter examines the excruciating pain of being unseen, and how the Fearless Dialogues team equips unlikely partners to see invisible persons and communities hidden in plain view. Central to this work are the age-old theories of William James and Howard Thurman, and the contemporary studies of Kipling Williams and Jane Vella. As educational environments can be sites for both personality development and identity assault, the following pages will draw us into classrooms for insight and introspection. In the imaginative company of blackboards, master teachers, and inquiring minds, together we will examine the fear of being "cut dead" and having one's self deemed unworthy of notice. Vella aptly calls this phenomenon the fear of "plopping."

A CUTTING SOUND: THE PERILS OF PLOPPING

Difficult to spell, but easy to understand, "onomatopoeia" was the longest word Ms. Flannigan taught us in third grade. The echo of comic-book sounds and farm animals rang in my ears as classmates yelled out words that imitated the natural sound of things. When I was an eight-year-old, "Boom!" "Oink," "Crash!" and "Moo" evoked laughter, innocence, and glee. Decades later, one onomatopoeic word triggers disdain and sizzles on my tongue like a four-letter expletive: "Plop!"

Imagine. . . . A single droplet of water forms on a ledge of New York City's Empire State Building. Against the backdrop of the new morning's sun, some 1,250 feet above the city street, microscopic water molecules gather in weight, in size. Trembling in resistance, the weighted driblet strains to hold on to the lofted ledge. But gravity takes its toll. The swift descent begins. Whizzing through the air the droplet gains velocity as it nears the sidewalked earth. It zeroes in on its target, a homeless man's plastic paint bucket weighed down by thirty-seven cents and two inches of rainwater from last night's thunderstorm. Moving at a speed nearly undetectable to the human eye, the droplet plunges into the paint bucket and belches out a deep-throated "Plop." Not a soul notices the sound echoing from the paint bucket except the homeless man awakened by the diving drop. With a thin piece of cardboard doubling as his mattress at the base of the iconic tower, he unfurls from his fetal-positioned sleep. As his eyes reorient him to his grounded space, he watches coffee-toting commuters literally step over him, as if he did not exist. Every morning the ritual of hard-bottomed shoes plopping against the unyielding pavement reminds him of horses galloping downhill to Hades. He is their angel, pierced in the side. But, in their eyes he is a faceless thing.

Who did you see? Who didn't you hear? Where is hope?

Jane Vella coined the term "plopping" in *Learning to Listen Learning to Teach: The Power of Dialogue in Educating Adults*. According to Vella, plopping is the fatal moment when an adult learner says something in a group and the speaker's words hit the floor without affirmation—or even recognition that she has spoken.[2] Plopping does violence to the speaker and the hearers, because others in the room may internalize fear and anxiety. After the initial plop, some onlookers may reason, "If I share my truth, it too may crash to the floor with no account." Plopping violates. Once heartfelt words hit the floor, the speaker is cut, the hearers freeze, and a crimson stain spreads, making the room no longer safe for authentic sharing.[3]

After prolonged reflection on Vella's term, a counterintuitive revelation emerged: Plopping induces fear and incites pain because listeners do not see the speaker. The fact that the discounted words are not heard is actually secondary to the speaker's pain. The primary wound of plopping occurs because the speaker is not seen by the listeners as worthy of recognition, affirmation, or notice.

In the opening vignette of this chapter, I describe my efforts to join the conversation in my first doctoral seminar. Seconds after tossing out my first words, I recognized the faces in the room going blank. With my ideas bouncing off the cellar walls and deadpan faces in search of receptive ears, it felt as if I was speaking into a vacuum, a hollow space. In that moment, the content of my researched comment mattered little. I merely sought a subtle cue—a raised eyebrow, a nodding head, a furled lip of disgust—to alert me that I was seen, that my truth was recognized. It did not come. But when I finished speaking, faces were enlivened, and the conversation continued as if I had not uttered a word. My words plopped. I sat frozen in disbelief, feeling like a faceless thing, unworthy of recognition, affirmation, or notice. The veil of invisibility fell fully on me when a classmate across the table repeated my comment and garnered validation from the group. Unseen in the eyes of my peers and professor, I felt a sharp pain sear within, and my five-year quest to be seen began.

My classroom plopping account is far from exceptional. In fact, the unacknowledged are all around us. They scream from shadows and whisper in the dark. But do we have eyes to see? *Do you?*

EYES TO SEE: THE UNACKNOWLEDGED ALL AROUND US

Far too often, "in the traffic of our daily round" we render others invisible. We step over homeless persons, as if they are of no account. We talk on cellphones in checkout lines, giving little notice to the grocer bagging our food. We even discount hypervisible politicians, pastors, and professional athletes by creating public personas that give them little room to express the fullness of their personalities. The unacknowledged are all around us, and if we are fully truthful with ourselves, we can each recall a fated moment when we felt unseen. We know the pain of plopping.

Social psychologist Kipling D. Williams supports this notion that the perils of invisibility do not discriminate. In his text *Ostracism: The Power of Silence*, Williams traces the pervasiveness of ostracism across cultures and time by charting ranges of exclusion—from formal declarations of government-sanctioned exile, religious shunning, and military imposed silencing to short time-outs imposed by teachers, unexplained silences, and averted eye contact in close interpersonal relations. In order to give ostracism a face and transform this intellectually abstract concept into an everyday reality, Williams calls readers to an exercise of remembering. Slowly read the passage below, and allow your soul to look back, lest you forget.

> Recall for a moment a situation in which your friends, family, coworkers, or relationship partners acted as though you did not exist. Remember feeling as though you were invisible, yet you could see the others going about their lives as though nothing unusual was happening. What did you do? Did you try talking to them to find out what was going on? But what if they didn't talk back, but instead acted as though they had not heard you? Maybe you waved your hands in front of their faces? If you did, what did it feel like when they looked right through them and you? What did you think when they even refused to make eye contact with you? Were you

able to carry on as though everything was normal? Did you start to withdraw? Or did you reciprocate their actions? Remember the time your family or friends made plans and everyone was included except you? Did you ask to be involved anyway, or did you disengage, wondering if you really belonged with these people anyway?[4]

Notice that Williams does not ask the reader to imagine these events. Rather, he calls his audience to remember them. He takes a well-calculated risk and presumes that every person has experienced an episode of ostracism in some form.

Recognizing that unlikely partners gathering for Fearless Dialogues conversations bear haunting memories of plopping, intentional efforts are made to see individuals as they enter and settle into the space created for hard conversation. As previously stated in chapter 3, through gestures of Radical Hospitality, Fearless Dialogues team members greet every unlikely partner with eye contact, a warm embrace, and our signature salutation: "It is good to finally see you. Welcome to Fearless Dialogues. Are you ready for change?" Experience has taught us that this brief eye-to-eye exchange can immediately transform a reticent onlooker into an engaged participant.

In June 2014, the Yale Center for Faith and Culture and the Yale Youth Ministry Institute hosted a Fearless Dialogues conversation around techniques to care for urban youth. To the delight and surprise of the hosts, nearly three hundred black and brown residents of New Haven gathered on Yale Divinity School's campus for this important conversation. Prior to entering the Living Museum, I stood on the old refectory steps to greet the incoming guests. With each unlikely partner, I connected eyes and offered the Fearless Dialogues signature salutation. In the throng that evening was an all-male prison choir slated to sing in closing worship. After my eye contact, customary welcome, and warm embrace, one choir member pulled me aside. With sincerity and passion glowing in his eyes, he disclosed, "I wasn't excited about coming here tonight, and I don't know what we are doing inside . . . but if you don't say another word, I already got what I needed. Thank you for taking the time to see me."

Recognizing the humanizing power of seeing, in Fearless Dialogues we foreground every session with multiple opportunities for eye-to-eye exchanges, small-group conversations, and high-impact mini-lectures about the perils of plopping and remaining unseen. In addition to examining theories of invisibility and recounting personal stories of plopping, unlikely partners are alerted to five fundamental human needs that are threatened when persons go unnoticed. This theoretical substructure provides a base to begin the work of equipping communities to see more clearly and hear more acutely unacknowledged persons in their midst. In the following pages, I pour the theoretical foundation for how Fearless Dialogues teaches unlikely partners to see the invisible. However, long before I possessed concrete theories to examine the detrimental effects of invisibility, my pupils had already been telling me something was not quite right.

PUPILS OF THE PIPELINE: DECADES OF QUESTIONING INVISIBILITY

Every morning that we pulled into the U-shaped driveway, my eyes drifted to the barred windows. On the days when we ran late, the line snaked out the door. At the front of the line, a standard salutation greeted each backpacker: "Any drugs, contraband, or illegal substances?" Once through the metal detector or the randomly selected wand searching, a cheeky backpacker would eyeball the ceiling, smile, and give the middle finger to the surveillance camera watching us enter. Up windowless stairwells, I walked to the second floor, found my desk, and waited for Dr. Hill's announcements.

But this was no ordinary day. For starters, Troy was not asleep at his desk. An uncustomary tension settled in the air. Suddenly, a voice boomed over the speakers. These were no ordinary announcements about the day's lunch menu or an upcoming school assembly. Unnerved words followed: "We are on lockdown! All teachers and students remain in your classrooms until further instruction." Within seconds we heard dogs scurrying through the hallways. One K-9 barked furiously in front of a locker just outside our classroom door. Before I could process the fullness of the situation, uniformed officers were handcuffing a classmate. As they carried him out the room, his grim eyes jolted me. The light behind his pupils dimmed. (. . . sigh . . .)

It all happened so fast. Yet somehow we were expected to return to business as usual. At that moment in tenth grade, a world I once viewed in Technicolor greyed. An emptiness began to fill my heart. By my senior year, I was so acclimated to the normalized chaos that I stepped around fights en route to the cafeteria like nuisance puddles on a crowded street.

Fortunately, in my overcrowded inner-city public school my teachers created safe havens in their classrooms for critical thinking skills to sharpen. By graduation, I had written five books, excelled in Advanced Placement courses, and found companionship in the writings of Dante, Chaucer, Du Bois, and Zora Neale Hurston. As a proud alumnus of Frederick Douglass High School, I firmly believe that I received a first-rate education. Surely I learned as much inside of the classroom as I did in the hallways hearing the storied lives of my peers.

But the grey-eyed emptiness from tenth grade still followed me as my unanswered questions lingered. Why was Troy allowed to sleep through first period every day? We all knew Troy "worked" at night. But was it easier for him to sleep through class than to receive instruction? What did people see in Troy? *Did they see him at all?* How do barred windows, morning searches, surveillance cameras, and building lockdowns ready students for college preparatory instruction? Or were my classmates and I being prepared for a destination that looked like the school in which we were challenged to learn? Did the taxpayers and school system who funded the infrastructure of our building see us as students? *Did they see us at all?*

In my secondary education, I articulated these questions but lacked theoretical resources to seek substantive answers. As a religion and sociology major at Emory University, under the tutelage of master teachers like Jaqueline Jordan Irvine, Bobbi Patterson, and Robert Agnew, I familiarized myself with literature on the school-to-prison pipeline, cycles of social neglect, and the potential impact of theory-practice learning. It was only then that I recognized that my chaos was not normal.

CUT DEAD BUT STILL ALIVE: MORE THAN MEETS THE EYES

In my nine years of schooling in New Jersey, I sought a new norm, to better understand the chaotic life of unacknowledged persons and communities. Against the daily grind of sustaining my own visibility and voice, I practiced paying attention to students, staff, and strangers on the street, all pressing for recognition and notice. Meanwhile, I steeped myself in studies of how mystics, martyrs, and seemingly marginal minority groups brewed hope in the midst of despair. This nine-year theory-practice loop of introspection, observation, and study had its onset in a course whose discipline was completely unfamiliar to me.

Never before had I heard of pastoral theology, a discipline that examined the inner world of the psyche and the contemplative space of the soul. But as an open-minded seminarian in my first semester of graduate school, I enrolled in a course titled Psychology of Religion. The course was taught by Donald Capps, a slim-of-frame and slight-of-voice professor in the twilight of his career.[5] While he was introducing Freud, Erikson, and Jung, students caught a glimpse of this prolific professor of quiet faith who loved poems, cars, and dry humor. In his lectures he infused religious melancholia and Christian hope into personal stories of his childhood days in Omaha, his formative years in Chicago, and his deep resonance with Malcolm X. Amid his run of storied lectures that semester, he tended carefully to the life and work of the famed American pragmatist and psychologist William James.

With James's highly touted *Varieties of Religious Experience* in one hand and a biography of James's life in the other, Capps peeled back the mask cloaked by the pseudonyms and poetic tropes in James's writing. As we cracked through the coded language and imagery, I noticed how James's personal life influenced his theoretical constructions of the "sick soul," "the divided self," and religious optimism.[6] Though lofted upon pedestals and heralded as the pillar of his field, in his writing James articulated his haunting feelings of invisibility and the fragmentation that occurs when persons remain unseen. In a final term paper for Capps's course, I stumbled across a bone-chilling James quote in *The Principles of Psychology*. His words articulated the phantom-like terror of invisibility and immediately gave clarity to questions I had started posing as a high-school sophomore.

> No more fiendish punishment could be devised, were such a thing physically possible, than that one should be turned loose in society and remain absolutely unnoticed by all the members thereof. If no one turned around when we entered, answered when we spoke, or minded what we did, but if every person we met '*cut us dead*,' and acted as if we were non-existent things, a kind of rage and impotent despair would before long well up in us, from which the cruelest bodily torture would be a relief.[7]

Fiendish. Punishment. Rage. Impotent. Despair. In a single paragraph, James's graphic accounting of invisibility gave shape, form, and language to a world I previously had known but struggled to articulate. Though penned in 1891, his words still felt relevant. His timely truths warranted a closer look.

Deep within James's 890-page tome, he argued that humans are social beings with an innate propensity to be noticed, and noticed favorably, by others. Conversely, going unnoticed or being cut dead is tortuous. "Cut dead" is a nineteenth-century idiom meaning to be ignored deliberately or snubbed completely.

Once I uncovered the meaning of James's morbid phrase, flashbacks flooded my consciousness. In an instant, I could see the cynical eyes of high-school classmates passing through security, the half-opened eyelids of the school-sleeping Troy, and the dimming pupils of my colleague carted off in cuffs. Unbeknownst to me, I foreshadowed my own fate as my corneas grew ever greyer in the cellared classroom of Princeton Seminary chapel. I dare not mention the reflections of myself I would see in the hollowed irises of the young men at Uth Turn. Yet, even with the greyness behind our eyes, light still flickered. So questions ensued:

1. What then of the ignored invisibles who hold fast to dreams and quest for hope?
2. In their own eyes, they are more than nonexistent things, so what measures will they take to gain notice?
3. If they still remain unseen in spite of efforts for visibility, will their rages boil and despair deepen? Will their dreams defer and hopes hamper?
4. Might other alternatives for visibility and hope lay over the horizon?

Gripped by these questions and the ones I had pondered since high school, I launched a seven-year quest to research how feeling unseen and unheard impacts the identity, future goals, and interpersonal relationships of African American young men. The culmination of this seven-year study was my first book, *Cut Dead but Still Alive: Caring for African American Young Men*. While grimly poetic, the book's title suggests that even when snubbed completely, hope can thrive in those who are "cut dead but still alive." This book chronicles the lives of six African American young men who struggled to hope in the face of invisibility and muteness. Since its publication, persons of different genders, ethnicities, socioeconomic backgrounds, and faiths have recounted story after story alerting me to the fact that being unseen and unheard is a human problem and global phenomenon.[8] Recognizing these anecdotal truths and Kipling Williams's assertion that all persons can recall, at some point, a time of being cut dead, at the onset of every

Fearless Dialogues conversation we introduce James's theory and challenge unlikely partners to wrestle with his age-old words.

Just days after the Fearless Dialogues conversation at Yale Divinity School, my colleague Alisha "Radio" Gordon and I animated a community conversation for youth at the 100 Black Men of America national conference. In the company of two hundred high school students and their mentors, we began our session by engaging James's morbid paragraph. After one brave high-school student read the passage to the two hundred gathered in the hotel conference room, we broke into smaller groups to discuss how these words made us feel. The thickness of James's words hovered as the youth and mentors processed reactions to the text. Minutes later, Alisha and I stood before the room and invited the unlikely partners to call out one-word descriptors of emotions evoked by the passage. As we quickly jotted the feelings down on white paper, with the power of gale-force winds, words like Anger, Rage, Hopeless, Insecure, Alone tore through the room. As lightning pierces dark grey skies, a shrilled voice cut through the room: "I feel suicidal."

Thunderous shock. Like the still winds in the eye of the storm, a hush covered the room. Through the young man's clouded pupils shone an all-too-familiar greyness. With the swiftness of relief workers after the levies broke, mentors triaged the young man and one trained caregiver rattled off the formulaic suicide protocol to ensure his safety. In the storm's aftermath, pupils refocused and fully grasped that seeing the cut dead is a life-or-death proposition.

A STRANGE FREEDOM:
FOUR FUNDAMENTALS OF LIVING
IN A CUT DEAD CULTURE

With tattooed teardrops falling from life-hardened eyes, the students at Newark's Uth Turn made it clear that they were willing to give their life (or take mine) in order not to be cut dead. Uth Turn was a program for young men transitioning out of prisons; so theirs was no ordinary classroom. Sans chalkboard, some sessions were held behind thick-paned glass, bolted metal doors, and narrow barred windows. Under the guard's gaze, I was slated to be their teacher. Or so I thought.

Need I mention again, these were no ordinary pupils. Hardened by gunplay, fallen friends, and an unforgiving drug culture, being seen as "soft" threatened their survival. So in seconds, the mildest plop or the subtlest slight of disregard could quickly explode into "in-your-face, see-me-now" posturing and escalate into a life-threatening altercation.

> Such posturing demanded respect, instilled fear, and guaranteed street credibility by threatening physical violence to anyone who disrespected, ignored, or belittled their humanity. The logic of this posturing posits that if you disrespect or ignore me, I will hit you (i.e., with my fist or with my gun) and you will "see me now."9

Though the young men I learned with at Uth Turn were willing to die to be seen as "hard," intuitively they understood that they were not being seen at all. Shielded beneath their urban exoskeletons lay compassionate hearts, untapped artistic gifts, and lofty vocational aspirations. Yet these qualities remained unnurtured, because they could not figure out how to escape punitive perceptions and life-limiting labels like "felon," "thug," and "dropout." Knowing full well the tensions of being wedged between the hypervisibility of stigmatizing stereotypes and the invisibility of shielded dreams, in one afternoon class I introduced the young men to Howard Thurman's elegy to the unseen, "A Strange Freedom."

Before handing out the five-paragraph, image-rich meditation, I asked them to close their eyes and think of the nighttime shadows cast by their cell bars. Then I whispered two questions into their remembered darkness: "Is it possible to be captive and free at the same time? Would that not be a strange freedom?" With opened eyes and furrowed brows, rivals began a discussion on freedom. Our stream of consciousness rushed over gang affiliations and around turf wars. But as the tension loosened, I raised the stakes for the sake of fearless dialogues: "If we are to speak our truth today, we must respect every person in the room as a learner seeking freedom from his chains. Some learn by hearing, others by doing, still others by reading . . . yet every learner has a teachable truth waiting to be taught. As we search for this strange freedom, can we all be learners today?"

As heads nodded, I felt the shame-inducing anxiety of some of the barely literate young men dissipate. Moments later, we broke into small groups and I handed out the meditation. With one strong reader in every group, I invited them to recite each word in every sentence slowly and deliberately. A cacophony of baritoned words rose to the ceiling, and before crashing to the floor they fell upon fertile hearts. My eyes scanned the room. Some read slowly. Others closed their eyes, sculpting mental images from the picturesque soliloquy. Nearly ten minutes into the exercise, the once-discordant voices took on the pitch, shape, and character of a meditative Gregorian chant. As the final voice trailed off into a contemplative quiet, the young men sat spellbound by Thurman's timeless truth.

Stepping into that solemn space, I encouraged the young men to identify the sentences or scenes in Thurman's meditation that most clearly defined their present reality. Group after group chose the same pericope:

> To be ignored, to be passed over as of no account and of no meaning, is to be made into a faceless thing, not a man. It is better to be the complete victim of an anger unrestrained and a wrath which knows no bounds, to be torn asunder without mercy or battered to a pulp by angry violence, than to be passed over as if one were not. Here at least one is dealt with, encountered, vanquished, or overwhelmed—but not ignored. It is a strange freedom to go nameless up and down the streets of other minds where no salutation greets and no sign is given to mark the place one calls one's own.[10]

Like Thurman, these young men knew all too well the felt reality of risking life and limb in order to be seen. Yet, for them, facing death for the sake of street recognition offered little freedom to live. A few articulated the captivity of labels like "felon"; others mentioned the numbing pain of muteness and invisibility. I can still hear one young man saying, "No salutation greets a thug . . . Just thug shit greets a thug." To be known by one's name, not by one's reputation or criminal record, is to be more than a faceless thing. While Thurman's "A Strange Freedom" plunged the readers and hearers into the depths of their inner world, vocalizing the emotions evoked from the meditation revealed deep and meaningful truths about the harmful impact of plopping and neglect.

That afternoon conversation brings to mind for me the work of Kipling Williams, who contends that four fundamental human needs—belonging, self-esteem, control, and meaningful existence—are threatened when individuals are unseen and unheard. In his studies on social ostracism, Williams chooses not to refer to these four needs as "desires" or "wants," because they are essential to human motivation and survival. Accordingly, when any of these needs are "lacking, people exhibit pathological consequences beyond mere temporal distress."[11] He further suggests "that these needs are peculiarly and almost immediately triggered by even short-term exposure to ostracism."[12] As these fundamental human needs are not mutually exclusive, all, in their own right, have the potential to wield a death-dealing touch. For this reason, I have come to liken each hampered human need to a rung of Dante's inferno, where the challenges of the previous circle compound the pain felt in the next.

Belonging

To be ignored, not dealt with or even vanquished by others, threatens one's sense of belonging. Perhaps the most fundamental of all human needs, belonging requires consistent interactions in a temporarily stable environment with a few people who are concerned for one another's welfare. Studies have shown that the need to belong is so important that without it "people suffer mental and physical illness, and are rendered incapacitated."[13] The strangely free and cut dead who stand in question of belonging may rightly wonder, "Who is my neighbor? Am I my neighbor's keeper? Does anyone want me as their neighbor at all?" In the wake of ostracism's deathly touch, three other imperiled needs shudder the infernal soul.

Self-Esteem

"Am I a faceless thing?" Reminiscent of Ralph Ellison's *Invisible Man*, being ostracized and overlooked sparks a negative internal dialogue that can debilitate self-esteem and eat away at one's intrinsic value. According to Williams, this corrosive psychic banter takes one of two forms. On one hand, the unacknowledged may feel that he is being ostracized because he has done something wrong. Without the benefit of conversation or visible recognition, this unacknowledged person generates a list of infractions that might warrant such unpleasant treatment. This growing list of plausible reasons for mistreatment threatens one's own perception of goodness and worth. On the other hand, the unacknowledged person may feel set apart and not acknowledged because of stigmas attached to deviance, physical appearance, or behaviors not accepted by the norm. In this regard, the ostracized one not only questions potential wrongdoing but also internally debates if he or she is desirable, wanted, or even capable of fitting in. Hence another question rumbles from the netherworld: "Am I flawed?"

Control

"A sense of control allows an individual to persist in the face of failure and to succeed."[14] Without control, that same individual may question, "Why do I feel trapped? Why do I feel targeted? Why do I feel bound?" If we cannot control being passed over as of no account, we have little power to shake the type-casting stereotypes others inscribe upon us. Researchers find that those who lack a feeling of control are susceptible to exhibiting learned helplessness or depression.[15] In the case of the young men at Uth Turn, even the potentially violent "see-me-now posturing" was a mirage of control, because striking out in violence further exacerbates the life-limiting labels the young men seek to escape. Trapped by an unsupportive community, bound by lessening self-esteem, and unable to control being passed over, the cut dead must cling for life.

Meaningful Existence

In the doldrums of the abyss, isolated and alone, tormented by internal banter, and stripped of control, the cut dead may ponder: "If I died today would anyone notice? After all . . . no salutation greets and no sign is given to mark the place I call my own." Being cut dead, deliberately ignored, and completely snubbed evokes this deeply visceral, emotionally wrenching existential question. Terror management theory argues that a fear of our own mortality and meaningless existence is a fundamental human anxiety that drives social behaviors.[16] If this is the case, persons who are muted and made invisible are forced continuously to contemplate the fragility of their existence and ponder whether their lives have meaning and worth.

Back to Thurman's Strange Freedom

Thurman's freedom is strange because it is not founded on liberty. To the contrary, the strange freedom of ostracism strips one of a face and a name, of meaning and worth. Such afflictions hamper fundamental human needs, spark tortuous questions, and leave the cut dead stammering through the hellfire in search of life-affirming answers. But thank God for the saints who have "ears that hear and eyes that see"[17] and those seeking freedom from estranging chains.

In the winter of 2013, just months before we officially launched
Fearless Dialogues, I taught a plenary session at a national ministers'
conference titled "The Unacknowledged Are All Around Us." On that
crisp January morning, nearly four hundred clergy in their Sunday's-
best suits and dresses filed into the hotel banquet hall, completely
unaware of the social experiment well underway in the Laboratory of
Discovery. Per custom, I began the session with eye-to-eye connection
and a standard greeting, "It is good to finally see you . . ." Following this introduction, we read William James's "cut dead" theory and
broke into groups of five to engage his emotive words. Lively chatter
filled the room, but one in the back row sat alone.

After charting reactions to James's theory, I called the church folk
to close their eyes and remember a time when their "friends, family,
coworkers, or relationship partners acted as though you did not exist."[18]
Once they opened their eyes, I invited them to share their guttural reactions in their small groups. The melodic sound of the memory-based
musings enveloped the hall, but the blue-jeaned fella in the back sat
silently with head stooped low. Following a minilecture on Kipling Williams's four fundamental human needs, I turned the ministers' attention
to the printed page, where they found Howard Thurman's "A Strange
Freedom." Each member of the group was asked to read one of the five
paragraphs. Much like the experience at Uth Turn, after minutes of
reading Thurman's words, the confusing cacophony of voices took on a
syncopated rhythm. But there remained one in the rear excluded from
this song; by now, he'd turned his back in sheer disdain.

Instead of fielding responses from the clergy who were clearly moved
by Thurman's words, I asked the blue-jeaned fella in the back to offer
his thoughts on "A Strange Freedom." In his approach from the rear,
he parted a sea of clergy to reach a microphone placed in the center
of the room. With each step, his well-worn tennis shoes contrasted
against their shiny wingtips; his hooded sweatshirt drew stares from
those in fine Italian suits. Once at the mic, he told his story of how it
felt to walk into a room "where no salutation greeted him" and where
he was "passed over as of no account." Nearly an hour had passed since
my eye-to-eye welcome, and not one person had invited him to join
a small group. Receiving no hospitality, he exclaimed that with each
passing exercise he felt more despondent, more like a "faceless thing."
Finally he disclosed, "My name is Minister Edwin Turnipseed. Dr.
Ellison is an old friend. He invited me here today and planted me on
the back row as part of a social experiment." As shock settled on the sea

of faces, he walked calmly to the back row and returned to the seat he had previously warmed.

Nearly an hour after I had shaken the last hand of the laudatory preachers, I received a call from my dear friend, Edwin. "Greg, would you believe that I walked out of that conference and not a single person spoke to me?" We rehashed the conversation about belonging, self-esteem, control, and meaningful existence. Then, as is our custom, we prayed for "ears that hear and eyes that see" the unacknowledged all around us, and the strangely free willing to give their lives for recognition.

A FINAL WORD
PREVENTING PLOPPING ON PARCHED LAND:
FOR FREEDOM WE SHALL LAY DOWN OUR LIVES

Far too many classrooms are desolate wastelands of creativity. These depositories of professorial wisdom render pupils as nomads, aimlessly wandering in search of earned credits, degrees, and awards. In such learning climates, the pursuit of collecting information dries out curiosity, and formation becomes a mirage. During my early years of graduate school, lecture-style classrooms left little room for dialogue, and far too many break-out groups exploded into fiery debate and competitive banter. With limited spaces for vulnerability and truth sharing, classmates sat in the company of peers like Familiar Strangers, largely unaware of the gifted souls sojourning with them.

Graduate school would teach me that like animals in the wild, "the soul is tough, resilient, savvy, [and capable of] surviving in hard places. . . . Yet despite its toughness the soul is also shy" and is reticent to show itself in spaces where others "preach and teach, assert and argue, claim and proclaim, admonish and advise."[19] In such a wilderness, where status, intellect, and ego supersede original thinking, curiosity, and respectful relationship, few brave souls expose their hides. Therefore, numbers of my graduate-school colleagues sought the haven of dense underbrush and found it safer to submit theoretically sound papers that safeguarded their souls rather than reckoning with the guttural realities of plopping, which might leave their souls open for slaughter.

Cautiously moving from underbrush to underbrush, I too trekked through the arid region of seminary in search of a flawless transcript.

On this quest to fulfill graduation requirements, the hard questions that drew me to theology school quieted, my desire to know was dulled, and my curiosity started to shrivel. The nomadic life was taking its toll, but before I fully succumbed to the status of an intellectual vagabond, I enrolled in a world religions course taught by an internationally renowned visiting professor.

The first day of class the formerly retired professor stood modestly before the chalkboard, pursed his lips, and spoke in a thick British accent, "This course is called 'Churches of Africa.'" Initially intrigued by the subject matter, I braced myself for the classes to come. Week after week, he lectured about Christian movements in Africa, but he never ventured beyond the eighteenth century. On the rarest of occasions, student questions were sought, and brief conversation ensued. By midsemester, my soul grew brittle like tumbleweed. I could no longer wander. Nor could I continue downloading places, names, and dates that I would surely forget well before receiving my sheepskin. So I made a bold decision that could easily land me a D– like the one I had earned in freshman chemistry at Emory. Choosing to wander no more, I carved out a solitary path.

Several evenings that semester I crossed the street en route to Princeton's Firestone Library. Hours passed as I leafed through primary sources. I sought further analysis in secondary texts. By day, I joined my classmates to hear lectures on ancient African churches, but my soul drifted to the historical accounts I read in the darkened carrels of Firestone. In my mind, I stood alongside young people who chanted, choked on tear gas, and tasted salted tears. On the final day of class, I thanked the demure professor who had lectured the previous twelve weeks on churches in Africa from the fifteenth to the eighteenth century. As my peers filed out of the classroom, they stacked their twelve-to-fifteen-page final papers in a pile on the front desk. Comparatively, my twenty-seven-page, copiously footnoted paper looked like a phone book atop the heap. Printed in bold letters like a protest placard, my paper title read:

> For Freedom We Shall Lay Down Our Lives:
> An Analysis of Structural Similarities in the
> Soweto Student Uprisings of 1976
> and the Protests of the Student Non-Violent
> Coordinating Committee
> during the Civil Rights Movement

Yes, you read it correctly. With scant reference to a single church, I wrote a twenty-seven-page paper about two student movements in the mid-twentieth century and submitted it for a class on African churches from 1400 to 1700.

For days, I braced for the impact of a near-failing grade. It never came. Instead, I received a brief note from the wise old professor. In short, he stated that he noticed when my demeanor enlivened midsemester. Even then, he wondered about the origin of my changed disposition. We never talked during the semester, so I was shocked that he perceived the shift. To my surprise, there was a "B+" at the bottom of the page. He disclosed that while my paper was among the best he read that semester, he could not in good faith issue me an "A" because the paper had absolutely no connection with the class. However, the passionate prose and careful historical research gave him a glimpse of why the light turned on inside me midway through the course. With wisdom and care, he saw my pupils aflame and chose not to let my truth plop. So he made a deliberate decision not to snuff out my intellectual fire with a punitive grade. That hard-earned B+ and his brief note forever altered my intellectual trajectory. With little more than a paragraph of carefully chosen words on the back page of my final paper, this old professor helped me to shatter the chains that bound my intellectual creativity.

Since this incident, I have pondered the unspoken pact between professor and pupil. That semester I studied the grey-haired historian more closely than the contents of the class. From day one, he created an atmosphere of routine predictability. On a weekly basis, he quietly arrived about seven minutes before class. When the second hand struck the hour, he began his lecture. With time-stamped accuracy, class ended promptly on the hour. He read his methodically researched lectures in a standard monotone; each one integrated historical artifacts, quotes from primary sources, and secondary analysis from interdisciplinary thinkers. However, for just a few minutes in each lecture, I'd notice a slight inflection in his voice, which provoked me to lean in and observe even closer. In these rare circumstances, he'd veer from his manuscript and speak of his personal travels to the places we were discussing. By midsemester, while many of my classmates sat in a dazed stupor, I waited in readied anticipation of his detour from the printed page. Having noticed his pattern, never once did I allow his seconds of truth sharing to plop.

In my nomadic space, the passion undergirding the unscripted words of his lecture felt like life-giving water for my soul. As my curiosity for learning was reawakened, my late night trips to Firestone grew more regular. The professor and I never spoke, but perhaps he recognized me gaining strength from his fervent diversions. For eight weeks, ours was a mutual dance of seeing between silent partners. After careful observation of his syncopated steps—research, analysis, impassioned speech—I wrote twenty-seven pages following his lead. With the hypervigilance of a thirsting apprentice, I awaited the weekly sightings of his inspirited soul. With the keenness of a sharp-eyed sage, he noticed my shy soul creeping from the sheltering underbrush, and he received my thoughts, convictions, and intuitions seriously. In each other's company, there was belonging, meaning, control, and bolstered esteem. Strangely freed from plopping, our creativity flourished. And together we quietly traversed parched lands by looking lovingly, facing hard questions, and listening for the sound of the genuine in the unacknowledged all around us.

5

Listening for the Love Below

Beyond the Fear
of Appearing Ignorant

With eyes aglow, the nocturnal animal emerges from the mouth of the cave. Just feet away from my fiancé and me, the metal beast growls out a warning cry. Doors swing open. We step forward. It swallows us whole. Within seconds, it pulls us into the shadowy caverns beneath the New York City streets.

Dozens join us in the belly of the beast. Faces unfamiliar. Humans of a hundred hues. Both pauper and professional whisked away beneath the surface to destinations unknown. Yet at that moment these unlikely partners roll together.

Against the oboish screech of spinning wheels, dissonant chatter and pregnant silence hang inharmoniously in the air. Standing in paint-stained jeans and hard-toe boots, a potbellied man speaking Italian shakes the hand of another rotund sojourner. Seated inches away, yet in a world of their own making, an Asian man with bejeweled hands and severe acne speaks in his native tongue to a younger counterpart. The novice zeroes in on every word dripping from the lips of the sage. Orbiting to their left sits the woman with the multicolored sweater, her eyes fixed vacantly on the ceiling.

Jolting stop. Doors fly open. Enter. Exit. 50th Street. Beyond the scratched paned glass of the mechanical beast stands a camouflaged soldier with bayonet in hand. Unfazed by the steady flow of evening traffic, his eyes dart around the dank cave scanning for suspicious activity, unattended bags. After all, the haze of fear still lingers thick in Gotham's air. Only sixty-eight days have passed since the Towers fell. Solemn darkness. Uneasy quiet. The beast pulses on . . .

I notice the finely dressed middle-aged blonde woman to our left, now surrounded by strangers, because her friends have stepped away. The softness of her cashmere coat contrasts with the textured leather bag she clutches closely to her chest. Her half-closed eyes flicker nervously. Not fully asleep, she closes out the unfamiliarity of this underground world and seeks solace in the darkness behind her eyelids. The fragrant smell of her Chanel perfume clashes in my nostrils with the pungency of the ruddy gentleman in ragged clothing lounging across the two seats before us. While no one seems to pay him mind, his eyes roam the corridor. As for the woman in the colored sweater, her eyes remain fixed on the ceiling.

Warning cries. Jolting stops. Flying doors. Exiting. Entering. 96th Street. We pummel northward on this Underground Railroad in search of freedom. Then there is a sound of another kind.

"I'm fifty-seven years old. I just left St. Luke's Hospital, where I stayed for sixty-eight days. On 9/11, I was stabbed outside the train station. I'm recovering, but I need help. Food, money, whatever you can offer." Homeless people seeking aid are far from rare in the belly of the beast. Just minutes earlier, a woman sauntered down the corridor soliciting donations in her tattered cup. She sat next to the ruddy gentleman in front of us. But something is different about his voice.

> what does this mean
> to see walking men
> wrapped in the color of death,
> to hear from their tongue
> such difficult syllables?[1]

As he approaches, I reach for my back pocket. Still on a student's budget, and with less than $30 on my person, I rifle through my billfold and, without looking, pull out the first greenback that greets my fingertips. In my foraging, the nervous chatter shifts to silence. The ruddy gentleman and the tattered-cup woman sit upright, the sage and novice shift their gaze, the sweatered woman's eyes descend from the ceiling, and my fiancé grabs my dollarless hand. "Are you really going to do this?"

With my eyes downcast, I lift the bill-holding hand from my seated position. But the recovering man will not receive the currency in his palm until I peer upward. Catching my eyes with his own, he responds, "Thank you." The silence is deafening, instructive.

His body collapses into a seat diagonally to our right, by the door. He pulls out a browning half-eaten banana, and before he takes a bite, his eyes find mine again. "Thank you." I nod my head in response.

Time slows to snail's pace. The baby blue and white tiles of the 116th Street station cascade outside the scratched paned glass. My fiancé and I stand and approach the metal doors. As the beast slows to a crawl, we cross the aisle. The banana-free hand reaches out and grabs my wrist. From a standing position, I glance downward at his reddened and watering eyes. In a faint whisper, he beckons, "God bless you, man. Thank you." Incapable of speaking, I nod again in gratitude for the ten-word lecture that changes my life.

Jolting stop. Flying doors. Swift exit. An entrance of tears. Class dismissed . . .

Once topside, I rushed to my fiancé's Harlem flat, and began drafting a term paper that my subway professor may never read. Over tear-stained pages, I recounted my semester-like journey in the belly of the beast, and the dramatic entry of my teacher. Unlike any course on Princeton's Ivy green, this night class felt liturgical in flow and in form. His invocational tone called forth attention. Like gospel, his authentic appraisal of affliction attuned the inattentive ear. As I searched in the contemplative quiet of his confession, hard questions emerged, prompting a sacrifice. I lifted a bill-holding hand. In proximity to the holy, I bowed low. Yet in his pedagogical sanctuary he beckoned me to lift my head and listen empathically with my eyes. Our "long loving look" in the sanctified silence was followed by a litany of thank-yous. More than a dozen years later, I script this chapter as a benediction, a sending forth, if you will.

As is true for good worship, lessons from that evening linger, and timeless questions persist. Who is my neighbor? Am I too fearful or ignorant to notice when strangers invite me into relationship? Am I even fit to be a neighbor, if I do not value strangers enough to offer human-to-human connection? In periods of discomforting silence, am I equipped with enough humility to receive wisdom and not fill the space with empty words? Am I prepared to welcome the probing presence of mystery both in spaces that seem familiar and around people who may or may not know me well?

The questions evoked from my subway encounter lifted a veil. On that evening over a dozen years ago, I drafted my first words on the psychology of invisibility. My interaction with the unlikely professor also revealed that shared vulnerability, authentic speech, and intimate connection require unmasking. Subsequent research and experiences in community conversations have led me to believe that the fear of appearing ignorant prevents such unmasking by cloaking our inner truths with insincerity. The false face of insincerity hides at least three insecurities:

1. I am unfit.
2. I feel unequipped.
3. I feel unprepared.

Any one of these insecurities can impair meaningful exchange. However, when compounded, these three insecurities harden into a mask that distances one from self and others.

In the pages that follow, I offer three strategies employed by Fearless Dialogues to chip away at the mask cast from a fear of appearing ignorant. The strategies to break this mold of fear are informed by interdisciplinary theories, interactive pedagogy, and critical introspection. Each of the following strategies is designed to peel away one of the three masking insecurities:

1. Increase proximity, to lessen feelings of being unfit.
2. Listen empathically, to dissipate the anxiety of feeling unequipped.
3. Inquire humbly, to diminish the voices of feeling unprepared.

In order to exemplify the power of unmasking, throughout this chapter I return to the opening vignette, draw from personal narratives, and recount moments of intimate connection emergent in Fearless Dialogues conversations. Lastly, I invite you, Beloved Reader, to wrestle with your own insecurities and fears of not knowing self and other. Piece by piece, together, let's pry off our masks and listen for the love below.

LESS THAN HUMAN, MORE THAN A GRADE: VALUE, DISTANCE, AND THE INSECURITY OF BEING UNFIT

At certain periods of the semester, a midday walk to the mailroom evoked the same terror as walking down an unlit back alley on the wrong side of town. As I jangled the keys before my graduate-student mailbox, even on the warmest days my blood would chill, my heart would race, and a cold sweat would trickle down my spine. With a clockwise turn, the key unbolted the lock and my breaths shortened. Inside the box, a graded paper. While I was familiar with the words I typed on the page, it was the blue- or red-penned comments of my professors that sent my soul a shiver.

On those blood-chilling, heart-racing student days, I unconsciously equated my worth with the subjective assessment of my professor. Therefore, if I received a B–, it ruined my day, because deep inside I felt less than adequate. I was unfit. While I sheltered these feelings of inadequacy with half smiles and head nods, parasitic self-doubt slowly ate away my sense of worth. Then one day a colleague taught me how to kill the parasite.

It was my third year of graduate school, and a disgruntled classmate from Jamaica stormed into the lunchroom looking for a place to vent. She sat across the table from me and unloaded. Enraged by an insulting interaction with a teaching assistant, her thick patois sliced through the noonday air. She shared with me her final response to the insensitive teaching assistant before she bolted from the classroom and into the dining hall. Her words I have never forgotten: "I may be from a third-world country, but I don't have a third-rate mind. And you will not treat me that way." Her statement was a declaration of value and personhood. The longer I sat with the wisdom of her words, the more I felt self-doubt flushing out of my entrails and my sense of worth returning. In time, I heard an echo rumbling from the deep: "I don't have a B-rate mind. I am not a B-rate person."

The lasting lesson from her outburst: neither teacher nor student was fully valuing the other as human. Both objectified the other, and neither was heard. The teacher-student relationships had devolved into transactional exchanges.

As a student, I valued my ideas, but attached far too much of my identity to the subjective grading of another. Therefore, in some cases I devalued my professors as persons and identified them solely as the purveyors of my grades. In other cases I overvalued my professors and their power to grade me, as the bearers of my future. Whether devalued as grading machines or overvalued as demigods with control of my future, professors to me ceased to be fully human. In my own eyes, we were cut from different cloths. Likewise, my patois-speaking classmate alerted me to the fact that some teachers fall victim to similar bias, projection, and objectification by deeming students who think, write, or respond differently as unfit.

"Unfit" means "not of the necessary quality or standard to meet a particular purpose." While far too many schools measure quality from the shoulders up, it is not only students and teachers in academic settings who improperly valuate others and display insecurities that they are unfit to meet necessary standards. In community life, perceived difference also creates a chasm between self and other. At Uth Turn, some devoted mentors with no criminal history deemed themselves unfit to offer counsel to street-savvy gang members. In the media, I witnessed aging activists consider millennials in Black Lives Matter disrespectful and unfit to carry their mantle of protesting injustice. In Fearless Dialogues community conversations, I have seen well-intentioned white folk fall silent on issues of race because they deem themselves unfit to speak on such matters in the company of black compatriots. Whether one projects unfitness or internalizes a lack of necessary quality, a fear of not knowing how the objectified other will hear the speaker's fact creates distance between parties.

I am reminded of my high-school shop teacher explaining, "To be ignorant is to be unaware of the facts." The fear of not knowing how others will respond to our unawareness scripts an internal dialogue of unfitness and stifles relationship development. Consider the internal dialogue of unfitness in the scenarios above. The student fears being labeled as not smart enough, so he overvalues the assessment of the professor. The teaching assistant fears not being in control enough, so he devalues the Jamaican student. The aging activists fear not being relevant enough, so they devalue the efforts of younger activists. The Uth Turn mentors fear not being street-savvy enough, so they devalue their own experience and withhold wisdom from the gang members. Well-intentioned white folk at Fearless Dialogues fear not being racially conscious enough, so they undervalue their own story and choose silence as a means of solidarity. Just beneath the surface of each of the scenarios is the supposition that someone is not enough. When we fear appearing ignorant and exposing to others an unawareness of facts, this valuates others and ourselves in ways that inhibit community building. To combat the parasitic feeling of unfitness that distances self from other, Fearless Dialogues increases proximity.

Who Is My Neighbor?: Increasing Proximity
to Lessen Barriers of Unfitness

Hazing is illegal, I've heard. But in a distant day, members of Black Greek fraternities could spot "the walk." This uncharacteristic gait of gingerly dragging one leg and mindfully walking down steps was immediately recognizable to other victims of pledging's posterior paddling. I've heard this walk develops when the soft tissue of the paddled posterior hardens and crusts over to protect the hypersensitive nerve endings. The masks we wear function similarly. Some blunt trauma challenges us to don a mask to protect the hypersensitive nerve endings of raw emotion and the soft tissue of the soul. Interestingly, just as other victims of pledging can recognize "the walk," strangers who have once disguised their soul can spot a mask from a distance. Such was the case with my subway professor.

With the sound of the cascading train doors closing in the background, I immediately discerned the authenticity and unmasked vulnerability of my subway professor's voice. When he stepped across the threshold into my three feet of space and refused to accept my greenback until I lifted my eyes, I believe he spotted something familiar in me. No way could he know the fright I felt days earlier when I jangled my mailroom keys to retrieve a graded paper. But perhaps he knew the heartache of devaluing self and overvaluing others. In a span of a few minutes our eyes connected, my feelings of unfitness were rescinded, and a stranger became a most unlikely neighbor who changed my life.

Under what conditions do strangers become neighbors? This query so troubled the thinking of sociologist James A. Vela-McConnell that he chose to examine how intimate ties of community form in an increasingly globalized world. His thinking is expressed in his aptly titled book *Who Is My Neighbor?: Social Affinity in a Modern World*. Drawing upon classical notions of social cohesion and contemporary theories in social psychology, Vela-McConnell explores how individuals and groups gravitate to others who share some social affinity. He suggests that the relationships patterning our lives are governed by varying degrees of affinity. On the surface level, affinity "indicates resemblance" and is apparent in connections with those who share similarity, likeness, or association. At a slightly deeper level, affinity "suggests fondness," where shared bonds are evident in closeness, affection, and attachment. On an even deeper level, affinity "implies kinship," and strong ties reflect a deep connection or unwavering union.[2] However, the question remains, Beloved Reader: How do we find resemblance, fondness, and kinship with strangers, when the ground of social affinity rests on an active fault line?

Vela-McConnell argues that far beneath surface-level affinity lie two shifting plates that crack connections with neighbors and crumble moral obligations to strangers: proximity and distance. In an increasingly globalized world, proximity and distance create tensions of attachment and detachment that complicate relationships between individuals and groups. Vela-McConnell describes the modern-day push and pull of connection and disconnection as "the paradox of the stranger":

> At the same time that we are in contact with ever-increasing numbers of people from all over the world, we feel more disconnected from those around us. At the same time that technology makes it possible for us to be informed of events happening across the globe, we feel increasingly overwhelmed by all of the claims upon our attention and sympathy. And at the same time that the world is brought virtually into our living rooms, the personal ties are still missing. We are caught in *the paradox of the stranger*—we are simultaneously proximate and distant with the world's population and even our neighbors.[3]

To more clearly understand this paradox, Vela-McConnell structures his work around three ways that individuals can be proximate and distant: spatial proximity, temporal proximity, and social proximity. As we will see, these three variables impact social affinity, how we value humanity, and our fitness to respond to the needs of strangers. As we reflect on these three variables, Beloved Reader, take stock of how space, time, and similarity affect your own relationships.

Spatial Proximity

Spatial proximity "pertains to the literal geographic distance between two or more individuals or groups."[4] People can be as proximate as passionate lovers or as distant as outliers from faraway lands. This physical distance between individuals or groups vastly influences personal contact, social affinity, and human empathy. In 1991, I recall my teenage mind wrestling with national news coverage of the opening battles of Operation Desert Storm. Under the cover of nightfall, nightscope cameras televised the aerial pyrotechnics that looked like neon green lasers knifing through the sky. Because war happens in regions of the world distant from the United States and I knew no one "over there" in Baghdad, the neon green lasers initially triggered images of video games and fireworks. However, the longer I sat before the screen, the more I reckoned with the decapitated limbs and incinerated bodies on the receiving end of the neon laser-like bombs. Do our capacities for compassion diminish as the spatial proximity between strangers expands?

Temporal Proximity

The second variable, temporal proximity, "refers to the amount of time separating two or more individuals or groups." This variable challenges us to think about our distance from forebears and our proximity to those not yet born. Temporal proximity underscores the notion that our individual and group decisions have both short-term consequences and long-term effects. "Are we aware of the consequences—either positive or negative—of our actions today for our own future and for the future of those yet unborn?"[5] In referring to the intergenerational nature of decision making, I recall my grandfather's adage, "We sit under shade trees that we did not plant and drink from wells that we did not dig." From his age-old wisdom, I gather that I am the manifestation of ancestral prayers and I reap the benefits today of backbreaking labor from yesteryear. Questions abound from this truth. How, through our decisions today, are we planting seeds and digging wells for great-great-grandchildren we may never meet? Do our short-term gains for upward mobility honor the sacrifices of our ancestors or create long-term pitfalls for future generations? Are we leaving the earth in a condition that will estrange our neighbors in years to come?

Social Proximity

The final variable, social proximity, references "the degree of similarity or dissimilarity between individuals or groups."[6] According to Vela-McConnell, these variants are revealed in at least two attributes. Ascribed attributes involve characteristics with which we are born, such as gender, race, ethnicity, and sexual orientation. Achieved attributes refer to characteristics that are earned through our own efforts, such as education, occupation, and social position.[7] For many people, the ascribed and achieved attributes of race, gender, and education affect decisions about who falls within our inner circles of neighbors, friends, and family and who can be labeled as one of "us." Likewise, those with fewer attributes to pull on our heartstrings of resemblance, fondness, and kinship are oftentimes relegated to stranger status and become one of "them." With a dearth of shared ascribed and achieved attributes, far too many of "us" may feel unfit to connect with "them."

In 2005, this matrix of attributes, social proximity, and binary categorization was thrown into a topspin when the toxic gumbo from Hurricane Katrina filled the Crescent City of New Orleans. Hours before the storm surge, I found myself on Princeton's campus studying for my doctoral exam on theologies and psychologies of hope. Yet I could not faithfully write about hope as despair flooded headline after headline. Rapt by the national news coverage on the aftermath of the storm, I was overcome by a sinking feeling. Then arose the empathetic epiphany: if I were sequestered in the ramshackle Superdome, or waved a white flag like my uncle who was found atop a tattered roof, in the eyes of many I would be just another brown-faced "refugee" in dire need, regardless of my Princeton education or middle-class social position. How do unlikely partners move beyond an us-and-them binary to foster empathetic connections where ascribed and achieved attributes lessen in importance?

As distance increases and individuals and groups become less spatially, temporally, and socially proximate, opportunities for meaningful engagement also diminish. In many ways, the subway professor and I were from different worlds. Though seemingly worlds apart, our paths fortuitously crossed at the right space and right time, to create an otherworldly social connection.

Indeed, we came from different spatial realities. I spent my days studying within ivy-clad buildings on the palatial grounds of Princeton, and on that night he roamed the urban corridor in search of basic needs to survive. Yet our paths crossed on a Sunday evening train.

Our temporal realities differed. As more than thirty years my senior, he had clocked many more miles on the odometer of life than I had. Yet our pasts and futures intersected at that present moment.

While we shared a common complexion, our social realities were dissimilar. Free from physical pain, clad in my Sunday best, and seated next to the love of my life, my only mental ache was performing above average in a top-tier graduate program. Walking solo with fresh wounds in disheveled garb, he ached for basic necessities. Yet somehow my upward trajectory met his downward curve and, while we were eye to eye, our incongruent attributes found common ground. The eyes are so important here . . .

A Long Loving Look at the Real
to Increase Proximity between Unlikely Partners

Back in 1989, a Jesuit priest named Walter J. Burghardt published a five-page article exclaiming that contemplation was under fire in church settings and the broader society. He argued that the waning of contemplative acts spurs utilitarian thinking and prompts trans-actional relationships. In such atmospheres devoid of contemplation, utility stimulates happiness, profit precipitates pleasure, and people or things are worthwhile only when they are concretely useful. However, Burghardt argued that happiness, pleasure, and worth can be read-ily accessible in ways that do not dehumanize and objectify.[8] Draw-ing from the wisdom of the Carmelite monk William McNamara, Burghardt proposed a contemplative practice called "the Long Loving Look at the Real," which heightens awareness of reality and places indi-viduals in communion with the Divine.

Captivated by "the Long Loving Look at the Real," Fearless Dia-logues adopted an experiment from a colleague that was borne out of a contemplative practice that thwarts feelings of unfitness, diminishes transactional relationships, and increases proximity between unlikely partners.[9] Prior to outlining the process of this experiment, let us consider the words "real," "long," and "loving look." These words correlate respectively to spatial proximity, temporal proximity, and social proximity.

According to Burghardt, contemplation must focus attention on the *real*. "The real, reality, is not reducible to some far-off, abstract, intangible God-in-the-sky. Reality is living, pulsing people."[10] How-ever, for many, the real is often dictated by spatial proximity, such that physical distance desensitizes compassion, numbs empathy, and stalls social action on behalf of others beyond my circle of influence. A reckoning with the real pushes beyond these abstractions of distance and challenges the introspective person to consider how all life, regard-less of proximity, is interrelated. From this vantage, all are "tied in a single garment of destiny. Whatever affects one directly, affects all indirectly."[11] Therefore, in a global village of mutuality, the peril of innocents on the end of neon bombs "over there" in Baghdad should pain me like the fallen tears of my own offspring within arm's reach. This is much easier said than done, you think. Just wait . . .

. . . But waiting is uneasy for many. For this reason, Burghardt advocated that the look at the real be *long*, "not in terms of measured time, but wonderfully unhurried, [and] gloriously unharried."[12] Far from inertia, an unharried look at the real is Sankofa-based. In ancient Akan folklore, the Sankofa bird is a time-bending symbol that melds present, past, and future. As you see in the image, the Sankofa bird body is facing forward, and its neck perches backward, while it focuses intently on an uncracked egg it holds in  its mouth. This symbol represents a people who are simultaneously moving forward, while looking back to the past in order to grasp wisdom for the future. When operating in spaces unbound by temporal proximity, minutes feel like hours, flashbacks offer wise counsel, and encounters with strangers seed wisdom for generations to come. But how do we slow the second hand in the race of life?

. . . *Look lovingly* and "allow your whole person to react to the real. Not only your mind, but your eyes and ears, smelling, touching, and tasting."[13] Wholly different from the fixed stare of Judas, a loving look is captivated by the real "nicks and dents and scars" of neighbors, strangers, and unlikely partners.[14] Suppressing the need to analyze, argue, describe, or define, this compassionate gaze stretches beyond ascribed and achieved attributes that foreground *dis*similarity. In the silent, space-shifting, timeless glow of long loving looks at the real, I have witnessed the most unlikely of partners suspend their fear of appearing ignorant and carefully lay down their whole heart in the presence of strangers.

The Long Loving Look at the Real: How It Works

We first invite the unlikely partners at Fearless Dialogues to participate in a transformative experiment titled "the Long Loving Look at the Real." Because a number of the persons at these community conversations are Familiar Strangers, the title itself evokes intrigue and anxiety. To offer reassurance, in measured tones we inform the unlikely partners, "We have conducted this experiment with gang leaders, corporate executives, and students discerning vocation. Countless numbers of those who have fearlessly faced this contemplative task have found it to be immensely transformative." As the nervous chatters lessen to a hush, we then invite those gathered to pair up and sit at a comfortable distance, facing their partner. With no tables, other chairs, or laptops in hand to impair connection between the two partners, we ask them to briefly introduce themselves and designate a Person A and a Person B in their pairing.

After explaining Burghardt's article and detailing each word ("long," "loving look," "real"), we offer detailed instructions for Person A to look lovingly at the real Person B seated before them for ninety seconds. Of course, this generates another outburst of anxiety and nervous chatter. Still in measured tones, we offer additional reassurances: "The eyes are a mirror; a gateway to the soul. . . . If you look deeply enough into the eyes of another, it is highly possible you will see yourself anew." A few balk at the idea of engaging in this face-to-face encounter, so we offer an alternate opportunity to look deeply into the eyes of a pictured image from the Living Museum on an easel in the room. For those who choose to move forward fearlessly, we provide a few more instructions: "We want this to be a safe experiment, so please keep your long loving looks above the shoulder. We also recognize that this is unfamiliar territory for many, and in this silent experiment laughter may emerge. At times, laughter occurs to move us to a deeper space." Finally, we invite Person A to request the permission of Person B to look lovingly at them in their most real state. Once permission is granted, the room falls silent. We count down, "Three, two, one," and the time begins.

After the time elapses, a deep sigh of relief lifts from the gut of those gathered, and we give thanks to Person B for receiving Person A's long loving look at the real. Following this gesture of gratitude, we regroup and Person B requests permission from Person A to look at him or her lovingly. With permission granted, a hush covers the room. A countdown ensues, and time begins. Once the second hand makes its final tick, we hear another sigh, and a final gesture of gratitude is offered. Then, for a few minutes of reflection, we invite the partners to consider three familiar questions: "Who did you see? Who didn't you hear? Where is hope?"

A response to the first question, "Who did you see?" during a community conversation of local leaders at St. Mary's Episcopal Church in Memphis, comes to mind. One unlikely partner shared with another, "In your eyes, I saw my mother." Such reflections of glimpsing relatives (some of whom are deceased) in the eyes of strangers are very common in this experiment.

The counterintuitive nature of the second question unearths hidden jewels of connection. Such was the case when animating a bilingual conversation of racially diverse leaders at a gathering in Manhattan hosted by Faith in New York. Suppressing a fear of appearing ignorant in the eyes of his peers, a white male shared with subtle alarm what his inner voice heard when looking lovingly in the eyes of a black man he did not know, "I didn't hear anger, rage, or fear. I heard acceptance." A thoughtful conversation on upending bias ensued.[15]

Finally, a personal account on the third question, "Where is hope?" We once animated a community conversation with a nationally renowned leadership incubator. Because there was an uneven number of pairings for the Long Loving Look at the Real, I volunteered to partner with one of the incubator's members. In debriefing with my partner, I shared that for the first several seconds I focused my attention on her right eye. However, in those few seconds, I felt a barrier preventing our connection. So I shifted my loving look to her left eye and immediately felt a warm reception. I shared this observation with my partner. Immediately, her head tilted in amazement, and her jaw dropped in astonishment. She then conveyed to me that due to astigmatism, she wore a contact only in her right eye, because her left eye needed no prescriptioned support. Until that moment, no one had looked long enough and lovingly enough to notice this very subtle difference in how she viewed the world. Within moments the contact-bearing right eye seemed to brighten with hope.

Even more eyes open when we conclude the experiment by contrasting the group's visceral reactions to the Long Loving Look at the Real with the guttural responses recorded minutes earlier when examining William James's cut-dead theory (discussed in the previous chapter). We begin this final step by asking, "How did it feel to look lovingly into the eyes of the real person before you?" With little hesitation, words like "uncomfortable" and "awkward" rise to the surface. Shortly thereafter, respondents share words like "affirmed," "whole," "peace," "visible," "fully human," "honored," and "in the presence of the Holy." In every setting, it is necessary to highlight that "the initial discomfort we feel in looking lovingly upon a stranger is necessary to reach the deeper level of affirmation and wholeness."[16] As this reality penetrates the substrata of the soul, we hold up the group's list of life-limiting reactions to William James's graphic accounting of being turned "loose in society and remaining absolutely unnoticed by all the members thereof."[17] With their own two eyes Fearless Dialoguers see contrasting lists.

> To be unseen is to feel Anger, Rage, Hopeless, Insecure, Alone . . .

> To look lovingly at the real is to feel Uncomfortable, Awkward, Affirmed, Whole, Visible, Fully Human . . .

Then we share this final word, which I learned from my eye-to-eye encounter with the subway professor: in a few timeless seconds of looking lovingly at the real, you can glimpse the divine, salve the pain of being cut dead, and find a neighbor where a stranger once sat.

In every community we have worked with over the past four years, the epiphanies generated during the Long Loving Look at the Real have created a BC–AD shift in the community. After gazing into the mirrored eyes of a stranger and seeing oneself, it becomes exceedingly hard to objectify, devalue, or dehumanize. Intriguingly, proximity increases. Unfitness diminishes. Unlikely partners huddle closer together, the second hand slows, and the hallowed ground is tilled for the sharing of hard questions that displace the tectonic plates of the soul.

BREAKING GROUND WITH OPEN EARS: INTELLECTUAL HUMILITY, EMPATHIC LISTENING, AND THE INSECURITY OF FEELING UNEQUIPPED

Interviewing for a tenure-track teaching position is torture. One particular exercise is a fiendish punishment. This exercise is known by many names, but at Candler School of Theology we call it the "press conference." In this format, the candidate stands before the faculty and fields deep and probing questions from persons of all disciplines. In my press conference, I stood behind the lectern as my future colleagues fired questions from every angle. I wrote down every question and paused to think, so that I could respond to each query thoughtfully, thoroughly. In the last minute, one faculty member posed a question, and I had not the foggiest idea of how to respond. In shame, I dropped my head, and this reply dribbled from my lips: "I could make up an answer, but

. . . frankly, I don't know." From that response, my impending doom seemed certain.

Staring down at the floor, I walked cement footed from the lectern, wondering why I admitted my ignorance so concretely. Though nearly immobilized by my admission, my mind raced for a response to the professors rushing in my direction to greet me before they sped off to their after-lunch responsibilities. Soaked in shame, with leaden legs, and with eyes downcast, I had no clue what to say, when esteemed Old Testament scholar Carol Newsom extended her hand. As I lifted my eyes, I said nothing and waited for her to speak. She pulled me in closer, so I could actively listen to her groundbreaking observation. "Greg, your final answer was a perfect ending. 'Frankly, I don't know' shows your intellectual humility." Not one for overstatement, she walked through the crowd of gathered colleagues and exited the room.

For years I have contemplated why my confession of not knowing evoked such a visceral response of shame, silence, and immobility. While the press conference was intimidating, I did not feel unfit. After all, I was a finalist for the job, and I bore confidence that my prayers and achieved attributes (my academic record, clinical work, and ministerial experiences) granted me spatial proximity to interview for the position. Heeding the advice of a mentor, I took my time to write down each query hurled at me, and I worked to answer each question as comprehensively as I could. However, my inability to field a reply to the final question prompted a paralyzing feeling that I was unequipped, that I lacked the necessary resources or qualities to succeed in the particular task.

Henri Nouwen counsels that many persons are conditioned to believe that "we are what we produce."[18] Doctors heal. Athletes compete. Professors, at least well-equipped ones, have answers. In systems designed for upward mobility, productivity is a measure of success. Therefore, doctors unequipped to heal, injured athletes without the qualities necessary to compete, and professors lacking the resources to field queries may be called into question. This temptation to produce and have all the answers "touches us at the center of our identity."[19] So, when we feel unequipped to demonstrate our productivity, shame, leaden feet, and downcast eyes will likely follow. Yet Newsom and Nouwen propose another path. Together they advocate for an intellectual humility that detaches us from knowing all, and opens us to deeper levels of awareness: empathic listening to self, others, and the Divine.

Active listening is not the same as hearing. While hearing is "the faculty of perceiving sound," listening is "giving one's attention to a sound." To listen requires intentionality and attentiveness. "Given all the sounds assaulting our ears, all the voices calling for our attention, not to mention all the chattering going on inside our heads,"[20] listening is far from a simple task, according to my pastoral-care colleague Karen Scheib. In the fifth chapter of her book *Pastoral Care: Telling the Stories of Our Lives*, Scheib outlines strategies for learning to listen attentively. For Scheib, listening is a form of reverence, as it potentially provides access to the holy place of another's story. She names a few impediments to approaching the sacred ground of another's truth. I will name a few:

1. *Anxiety* impedes listening deeply to one another. In our quest to produce answers and results, we may limit our attentive listening and rush into speaking, in order to ease feelings of discomfort.[21] The most torturous press conferences, I have observed, are those in which jittery candidates fail to listen and sidestep questions.
2. *The roles we occupy* also impact how others share their story. Many pastors know the immense responsibility of listening to heart-felt concerns of struggling couples during premarital counseling. These same pastors know the feeling of being unwelcomed at that same newly married couple's wedding reception because of the clerical role. When bottles start to pop, loved ones may not want the pastor around when the spirits start to speak freely.
3. A final impediment is *our own story*. "Because we listen through our own story, there always lies the possibility of misunderstanding," especially in the company of persons who are different.[22] My subway professor asked for a basic need, which I misunderstood to be money. When he refused to receive the greenback, I was forced to listen more closely and recognize that his basic need was not monetary. It was to be seen.

To circumnavigate these types of impediments, Scheib teaches her readers to differentiate factual listening from empathic listening. *Factual listening* is a byproduct of what she calls "paradigmatic knowing," a form of logical reasoning deduced from our five senses to comprehend the nature of objects in the world. Such knowing is manifest through empirical discovery, the scientific method, and well-formed arguments. Factual listening requires knowing enough to produce well-formed arguments, accurately assessing the problem, and determining the appropriate solution.[23] Professors and students are not the only persons who engage in factual listening. "When asking for directions, catching the newscast, or listening to a doctor's diagnosis, we listen for information, and may ask questions to get the details clear."[24]

Factual listening is essential to navigating society. However, the human experience is both scientific and artistic, and some of life's hardest questions and most meaningful truths cannot be deduced from formulaic assessment and systematic argumentation. In order to receive certain types of wisdom, there are times when we must be pulled in closer to listen empathically.

Empathic listening does not have the ultimate aim of giving advice, solving another's problem, or assigning a diagnosis.[25] This form of listening emerges from cognitive and affective understandings of empathy. Cognitively, empathy requires "imagining ourselves in the midst of the multiple dimensions of another's experience in order to understand it."[26] Affectively, empathy challenges us to "step into another's shoes," imaginatively connect with our emotions, and attempt to feel what the other person is feeling.[27] When held in concert, the cognitive and affective dimensions of empathy provide "an emotional resonance through which we make a connection between another's experience and our own."[28] Empathic listening, Scheib teaches, requires equal parts connection and separateness. In this regard, the listener is challenged to be absorbed in the story of the other, while acknowledging one's own distinct feelings, thoughts, and differences from the storyteller. This paradoxical interplay of deep investment without overidentification safeguards the listener from paternalistic sympathy or a domineering imposition of one's own desires.

Empathic listening dismantles feelings of being unequipped by assuring the speaker that more is heard than is actually said. On the subway, following my professor's invitation, I felt unequipped to produce more than money. However, I know now that looking lovingly and receiving his gracious litany of thank-yous was more meaningful than any word I might have uttered. Likewise, immediately following the press conference, Newsom moved within the orbit of my gloomy sullenness and reassured me that she empathically listened to something that my spoken words of not knowing could not fully articulate. In both of these examples of empathic listening, only a handful of words was exchanged. Even more impacting were the hard questions that surfaced from the deep.

Fearless Dialogues recognizes that these two types of listening structure many conversational exchanges. While factual listening remains imperative to solve many of life's perplexities, empathic listening is necessary when receiving the invitation to enter into another's pain without having answers. To this end, we have developed an experiment that alters the topography of listening, so that unlikely partners empathically trek together the uncharted terrain of the five hardest questions we all face in life.

Penetrating the Crust with Circles of Trust: The Five Hard Questions Explained

As a child, old folk used to tell me, "You done been here before." The same could be said of the nine-year-old sage Saheim Hersey. In a recent course I taught titled Care of Souls, Care of World, Saheim's mother found it fitting to interview her old-souled son for a class project. When faced with the daunting question, "What is the soul?" Saheim moved to the edge of his seat. After a pregnant pause, he responded with the sagacity of ages past. "The soul is like the inside of the earth. There are four layers to the earth—the mantle, the crust, the outer core, and the inner core. The soul would be the inner core. It's the most beautiful and powerful part of your body."

If Saheim is right—and I believe he is—the soul, like the core, is buried deep beneath layers of life, learning, and lived experiences that language cannot fully articulate. This nucleic core is our inner teacher, always ready and alert to guide us through confounding perplexities, if approached with honor and reverence. But unearthing the wisdom of the soul necessitates great care.

Recognizing that excavating soul wisdom requires the precision of an archaeological dig, Fearless Dialogues adapted an experiment from an age-old Quaker practice that cultivates empathic listening, roots out fear, and exhumes intimate truths from the core. In *A Hidden Wholeness: The Journey toward an Undivided Life*, Parker J. Palmer introduces a process of communal dialogue called "circles of trust." Palmer discovered this practice in the mid-1970s at Pendle Hill, a Quaker living-learning community near Philadelphia. Circles of trust are intentionally formed spaces that welcome the inner voice of the soul to show up and offer its guidance. More specifically, Palmer explains, "a circle of trust holds us in a space where we can make our own discernments, in our own way and time, in the encouraging and challenging presence of other people."[29] Let us first consider five guiding principles Fearless Dialogues has incorporated from Palmer (and his fellow Quakers at Pendle Hill). These guiding principles inform how Fearless Dialogues crafts communal spaces for asking hard questions, listening empathically, and inviting the inner teacher of the soul to show up as a guide.

1. The inner teacher of the soul exists in all of us; so, when the student is ready, the inner teacher will teach. Through socialization, hardship, and conformity many of us have come to distrust, ignore, and even mute the soul's voice. As a result, we are disconnected from truths hidden beneath layers of insecurity. But occasionally our nucleic core will shift the plates and send tremors of epiphany through our being to remind us the soul still remains deep within. Though we may feel disconnected from our soul's story and have difficulty in recognizing its voice, our inner teacher faithfully awaits our invitation for tutelage. Unlike any other voice, the guidance that emerges from bedrock is far more "reliable than anything we can get from a doctrine, ideology, collective belief system, institution, or leader."[30] When the inner teacher emerges, its truth penetrates both the speaker and the listener, for this voice is authentic, unmarred, and holy. This genuine sound emerges when the speaker is readied and the conditions are set.

2. The inner teacher speaks when honored, not invaded. Palmer also speaks of circles not bound by trust that are unsafe for soul surfacing. Some circles are "thinly disguised exercises in narcissism and self-congratulatory piousness,"[31] while others are designed to direct or demand a certain outcome.[32] Honoring the inner teacher of the soul requires showing up with no other intention than to welcome it. When we create a space where the soul feels safe enough for individuals to speak fearlessly from their center, the inner teacher invariably instructs us how to deal with some of life's most divisive personal and social issues. In Palmer's circles of trust and Fearless Dialogues' Five Hardest Questions, we have observed souls unbound by outcome disentangle complex individual and communal contentions on matters like race, class, and identity politics.[33]

3. When fearless speakers communicate from their center, the ground of conversation quivers. As mentioned above, most

everyday conversations are paradigmatic and help us to make logical deductions to navigate the world. These conversations may be driven not only by intellect, but also by ego, as we consciously and unconsciously seek to demonstrate our productivity to others. Speaking from the center sheds the need to prove oneself, and opens one to receive creative insights surfacing from the unpredictable inner teacher. Centered speech also has a different tone than everyday banter, and for this reason we need fellow sojourners to help us decipher this messaging.

4. We need the support of fellow sojourners to listen empathically and to help us discern the inner teacher's voice. In the words of Palmer, "the path [to our core] is too deeply hidden to be traveled without company: finding our way involves clues that are subtle and sometimes misleading, requiring the kind of discernment that can happen only in dialogue."[34] This company of sojourners need not be large, but it must be willing to listen receptively and empathically. Such listening allows brief, reflective silences that honor the speaker and alter the pace of conversation for spoken truths to be absorbed. This type of listening further responds with honest open-ended questions, not critiques, commentaries, or simple fixes.[35]

5. Skilled leadership is necessary to prepare the ground for the soul to speak in a circle of strangers. Long before unlikely partners gather, skilled animators must fearlessly face life's hardest questions in a trusted circle of their own. In Fearless Dialogues' condensed format of the circles of trust, the lead animator invites the souls of unlikely partners to speak by modeling vulnerability. In such modeling, the lead animator shares brief accounts of a long journey in wrestling with these hard questions in a community of reliable others. The animator is called to claim and use past failures, fears, and inadequacies as instruments to build hope and trust in the process of facing life's hard questions.

This form of animation is equal parts art and science. Like walking a tight rope, creating a space for the soul to speak requires great balance and bold acceptance of risks. In this process, the animator walks a thin line: if you share too little, you model a concealment and trepidation that stifles intimate truth sharing; if you share too much, you model narcissistic grandstanding that clamors for attention and drowns out the genuine sound of the soul. To be clear, the demanding and rewarding role of a skilled lead animator cannot be taught in a book. For this reason Fearless Dialogues has designed a face-to-face animator preparation program.

These guidelines serve as the foundation for Fearless Dialogues' one-hour condensed version of the circles of trust. Acknowledging, honoring, and inviting the inner teacher is the subflooring for a soul-friendly environment where unlikely partners speak intimate truths from their center. Like support beams, fellow sojourners prepare their hearts and minds to listen empathically and receptively to discern the inner teacher's wisdom. Finally, skilled animators frame Fearless Dialogues' Five Hardest Questions by modeling vulnerability. However, this entire structure of deep conversation collapses if we fail to build in the practice of humble inquiry.

SCALING THE DEPTHS: HUMBLE INQUIRY, MYSTERY, AND THE INSECURITY OF BEING UNPREPARED

Deep sea. Deep space. Deep earth. Placing the word "deep" before these three nouns conjures images of the mysterious unknown. Oceanographers tell us that after centuries of study, scientists have explored only a tenth of 1 percent of the ominous deep sea.[36] Astrophysicists recently deduced from Hubble Space Telescope data that there are almost two trillion galaxies in the universe, but more than 90 percent of these galaxies in deep space remain unstudied.[37] Geoscientists, still puzzled by deep earth, continue to pioneer pressure-generating technology and new techniques for measuring sound velocity, so they can study the earth's core that heats up to 8,500°F and is nearly four thousand miles beneath the ground we walk on.[38] Like the sea, space, and earth, deep conversation can awaken mystery and arouse humble inquiry.

Early in my teaching career, I failed to offer necessary deference to mystery and credence to questions. Insecure and fearing that my students would find me unprepared for class, I crafted phonebook-sized syllabi, drafted (and delivered) lengthy lectures, and shafted far too many opportunities for exploratory conversation. My fears of appearing ignorant before students prompted me to overprepare and to underutilize the wealth of wisdom in the room. This overpreparation stunted discovery, because I offered students solutions without inclusion of their questions. In retrospect, my glut of prepared information eclipsed unknown galaxies of formation that might have emerged from humble inquiry and deep conversation.

Then one afternoon, in a basement classroom of Emory's Cannon Chapel, I learned to bow at the feet of mystery. With an eight-page outline in hand the students listened attentively as I examined the intersections of Carl Jung's depth psychology and Howard Thurman's mystical theology. Reading between the lines of the theorists' isolation and internal unrest, and intuiting an unspoken tension in the words of my lecture, a first-year student named Georgette Ledgister raised a question about disciplinary liminality: "Dr. Ellison, how does it feel to be a problem?" Immediately, a lump in my throat dropped deep into my belly, and a guttural sigh emerged, as her question settled in a mysterious space I had yet to fully explore.

In that moment, I realized that my weeks of careful research could not have prepared me to field her query; only my life could. Then a response bubbled up, "While this question rings true, I've never articulated a response. Might we work together and see where the Spirit takes us?" For the next thirty minutes, Georgette, her classmates, and I entered into a successive cycle of question and response. With each revolution of humbly posed questions, both student and professor descended deeper into the unknown territory of the inner world.

Georgette invited me and her colleagues into a space of self-discovery by gently asking a hard question that Edgar H. Schein would classify as a "humble inquiry." In his book *Humble Inquiry: The Gentle Art of Asking* Schein defines this type of query as a fine art of drawing someone out by asking questions to which you do not know the answer.[39] From decades of consulting and teaching at the MIT Sloan School of Management, Schein attests that the art of asking the right question in the right way can build relationship, solve problems, and move stymied conversations forward.[40] However, Schein acknowledges that building relationships through asking questions is countercultural in a society framed on telling.

Telling forestalls relationship building because it implies the other person does not in some way already know what is being said. Out of my insecurities as a novice professor I overprepared in order to appear productive. Yet I failed to consider that telling volumes of information in a carefully scripted lecture with limited space for questions might insult my students' intelligence. In a culture where telling is normative, and not knowing may appear as a profession of ignorance, asking requires risks and vulnerability for professors, students, and unlikely partners.

Asking, as Schein informs, has the potential to honor the questioned, invert hierarchies, and build relationships. Asking honors the person being questioned by implying that the other person knows something of such value that I am willing to listen and to make myself vulnerable to learn.[41] Inferring that others possess valued knowledge worth asking about grants someone a higher status. This hierarchy may seem inconsequential when a student asks a professor, a child inquires of a parent, or an employee questions a boss. But when the tables turn and the questioner is perceived to possess a different achieved status, a deep reserve of humility is required. This back-and-forth of humble asking generates relational bonds, as both the questioner and the questioned recognize a mutual investment to share and learn. However, not all asking is created equal.

Humble inquiry, circles of trust, and the work of Fearless Dialogues are grounded in the posing of honest, open questions. "An honest question is one I can ask without possibly being able to say to myself, 'I know the right answer to this question, and I sure hope you give it to me.'"[42] Open-ended questions convey curiosity and sincere interests (through body language, tone of voice, and timing) in the other person.[43] These types of questions invite exploration and welcome the inner teacher of the soul, instead of nudging (or forcing) the speaker into a particular response that benefits the questioner. Consider the following examples documented in Palmer's *The Courage to Teach: Guide for Reflection and Renewal*:

Closed question: Have you thought about seeing a therapist? Here, we find advice cloaked in question's clothing.

Honest question: Did you learn anything from that prior experience that feels useful to you now? With no way to imagine a "right answer" this query invites the soul to speak its truth.

Open question: How do you feel about the experience you just described? Like the honest inquiry above, this question opens gateways for authentic sharing.[44]

In summary, honest, open questions communicate a willingness to listen and invite the speaker to tell you more. Closed questions shut down conversation by attempting to fix or by prompting fact-based yes or no answers. Posing honest, open questions requires the discipline of "minimizing our preconceptions, clearing our mind at the beginning of the conversation, and maximizing our listening as the conversation proceeds."[45] Sidestepping the potholes of closed questioning requires resisting the temptation to advise or fix.

When people garner the courage to reflect on their deepest questions, they are not seeking to be fixed or saved: "they want to be seen and heard, to have their truth acknowledged and honored." Yet far too often in soul-deep moments, the listener's insecurities of feeling unprepared or unequipped trigger an impulse to fix the speaker. However, empathic listeners and honest, open questioners must resist this temptation. "The human soul does not want to be fixed, it wants simply to be seen and heard."[46] Therefore, we must not rush to repair and sidestep the important process of seeing and hearing. Clearly, not every traveler and unlikely partner is prepared for the long loving descent into the inner world. Yet there is a process we employ for those willing to take the hike.

Down into the Mountain Crevasse: The Process of Asking Hard Questions

The Fearless Dialogues process is an emotionally grueling trek. At the parking lot or front door, animators, like Sherpas, extend Radical Hospitality at the base of the mountain. To gear up for the climb, unlikely partners take name tags that label their gifts. On the measured ascent to base camp, unlikely partners consider three questions in the Living Museum to acquaint themselves with the unfamiliar terrain they have committed to scale. Once at base camp, animators and partners covenant to lift as they climb. As the treacherous climb begins, the unlikely partners seek a foothold on William James's cut-dead theory and find a firm grip on times in their past when they felt invisible. As the pitch steepens, the air grows thinner, and the climbers must face insecurities and fears. At this moment, unlikely partners recognize the value of fellow sojourners, and in close proximity they take a long loving look at the real. But the inner teacher may not always appear on the incline. Sometimes in scaling mountains, we must traverse the crevasse in pursuit of the summit. On the descent into the deep crevasse of the soul, Fearless Dialogues calls upon animators and unlikely partners to gather in circles of trust, inquire humbly, and face life's five hardest questions.

By utilizing strategies for empathic listening, crafting circles of trust, and teaching humble inquiry, Fearless Dialogues created the following process to welcome the inner teacher and pose the Five Hardest Questions. I convey these instructions to you, Beloved Reader, as I have done dozens of times with leaders in communities across the United States and beyond.

Let us start the climb:

We call this experiment the Five Hardest Questions you will face in life. A couple of years ago, I had the opportunity to speak at career day to a second-grade class. In describing to them my role as a professor and vocation as a lifelong learner, I shared, "I have been in school for over thirty years." One of the spry second-graders responded, "Ooh, you're dumb!" For many years of my schooling, his assessment was correct. I had the privilege of learning alongside some of our country's sharpest minds in the Atlanta public schools, Emory University, and Princeton Seminary. I sat at the feet of master teachers and studied in libraries with thousands upon thousands of books. But more often than not, I found myself obsessed with finding answers. A dumb approach, I soon learned.

Over those same thirty years, I spent time with my grandparents. On Sundays, I sat on Granma's pew surrounded by church ladies with big hats. After church, I reclined on the porch with my granddaddy and his friends. I drank my lemonade as they swapped stories and told tall tales over strong drink. In time, I learned that careful listening and asking questions were paths to discovery. Answers were only part of the journey. To descend into the crevasse, I had to live and love the questions.

In speaking to his apprentice, master teacher Rainer Maria Rilke begs his pupil, "Have patience with everything that remains unsolved in your heart. Try to *love the questions themselves*, like locked rooms and like books written in a foreign language. Do not look now for the answers. They cannot be given to you because you could not live them. At present you need to *live the questions*. Perhaps you will gradually, find yourself experiencing the answer, some distant day."[47]

Like my grandparents and the books calling forth from the library shelves, Rilke beckons his student not to rush hastily into easy answers and simple solutions. Instead, he challenges the apprentice to recognize the value in patiently living into the unsolved mysteries of life.

In a few minutes, I will introduce a process that calls forth the soul to teach us. But do you have the patience to live and love the questions?

This is our task. This evening, I will introduce you to five hard questions that I have encountered through countless hours of study in hallowed halls of learning and on back pews and front porches with kinfolk I love. This is not an exhaustive list, but the questions increase in difficulty. I invite you to live into them and to love them with me and the partners in your circle.

We have invited you to sit in small circles of five. Notice there are no tables between you. If you have papers or pens, we invite you to put those under your chairs. We want nothing to stand between you and your neighbor as we face these questions. While we encourage each of you to remember your covenant to support your partners, at any moment if these questions become too burdensome, please feel free to excuse yourself. No judgment will be placed upon you.

This experiment is an exercise in empathic listening, humble inquiry, and a derivation of an age-old Quaker practice. [I then describe these tenets.] There are five people in your group and there are five questions I will pose. Each person is encouraged to answer one of the five questions. As the lead animator, I will introduce each of these questions to you by sharing a brief narrative of my encounter with the question. [Recall the tightrope that a skilled animator must walk in framing these questions.] While I am framing my narrative, listen attentively for the whisper of your inner teacher. Is she pulling you to the center to share your truth? If you feel the gentle nudge to respond to the question after it is framed, please speak your truth from your center for three minutes. Now, bear in mind this is an exercise in empathic listening. So, as one person responds to a question from their center, the other four partners in the group will sit in silence and listen with sincere interest. The four listeners have the immense responsibility of walking with the fearless speaker into the deep and helping to discern the inner teacher's voice.

After three minutes of truth sharing, I will ask the entire room to enter into thirty seconds of silent contemplation. These brief, "reflective silences honor the speaker and alter the pace of conversation for spoken truths to be absorbed."[48]

While the speaker's truth seeps into the souls of the listeners, I invite the four listeners to discern the spoken wisdom and wait patiently for an honest, open question to arise from their core. Then I offer a brief explanation of honest, open questions. When the thirty seconds expire, I invite the four empathic listeners to pose their honest, open questions. I tell them, "Be careful not to tell, advise, or fix, but view your humble inquiries as guideposts to help the fearless speaker on their journey." This is an exercise in reflective listening; so as humble inquiries are spoken to the center, I urge the fearless speaker to resist the impulse to answer. "No, we must live and love the questions." Following the questions, we give thanks for the speaker's authentic sharing and move to the next question.

Now we have a quick review. For each of the five questions we repeat this sequence:

1. The animator briefly frames a question.
2. A fearless speaker responds to the question for three minutes.
3. When the three minutes are up, the room will enter into thirty seconds of contemplative silence.
4. In this waiting moment, listeners absorb the shared wisdom and search internally for an honest, open question that might serve as a guide for the courageous speaker.
5. When the thirty seconds of silence are up, the four listeners will share their honest, open questions, and the speaker will receive these humble inquiries as gifts for the journey.
6. Finally, we give thanks for the speaker and the receptive listeners, and we move to the next question.

With the ground rules set, I pose one preliminary query before the Five Hardest Questions: "Are you scared? Don't be. Your souls have been waiting for this moment for quite some time."

Question 1: Who Am I?

"Who am I?" seems easy enough, but when you ask this question, others quickly follow. Who am I not? Who am I when the shades are drawn and the lights are off? Have I worn a mask so long that I cannot differentiate who I am from who "they" say I should be? If I know who I am, then what do I call myself? What do I call myself? I pose this inquiry to all first-year students in my classes, because the world can call us all kinds of names. I recall one student's response. "Once I came out of the closet, . . . my family kicked me out. They called me 'Shameful.' My church kicked me out. They called me 'Sinner.' My friends kicked me out of their circle. They called me all kinds of names. But on this first day of seminary, I call myself 'Free!'" What do you call yourself? Who are you? Who are you not?

Beloved Reader, take some time now and have a fearless dialogue with yourself.

Three minutes . . . thirty seconds . . . humble inquiry . . . gratitude.

Question 2: Why Am I Here?

Not, why are you here? Not, why are you here at your desk, in this coffee shop, in a library reading this book? No. Why are you *here? here? here?* Some split-second decisions were made so that you could be here and not somewhere else. Recall that moment when you could have followed the crowd, but you turned the other way. So, now you are here, and they are there. How did you get here? Somebody sacrificed so you could be here. Somebody worked long hours and prayed all night so you could be here. So, what are you gonna do, now that you are here? Granddaddy used to say, "We sit under shade trees we did not plant and drink from wells we did not dig." So, are you planting trees and digging wells while you are here? Or are you here just to be here? Why are you here?

There is a reason your inner teacher drew you to this page at this time. Live and love the question while you're here.

Three minutes . . . thirty seconds . . . humble inquiry . . . gratitude.

Question 3: What Is My Gift?

Far too many of us live our lives cloaking our gifts with talents ascribed to us by others. Then there are some of us who believe we have no gift. I recall my old friend and fellow animator Floyd Wood posing this question to a room of two hundred testosterone-filled black and brown teenage young men in Florida. In one circle of five, a meek young man responded, "I have no gift." The burly football player across from him would not let the meek lad off the hook so easily. The footballer questioned, "What are you good enough to teach?" The slight-of-build, shy young man mumbled back, "Tennis." "Are you good enough to teach me?" the football player volleyed back. "Sure," he mumbled. "Then your gift is teaching." The floodgates opened, and tears flowed . . . and flowed . . . and flowed. For five minutes these two young men stood in the center of a testosterone-filled room hugging and crying. It was the first time the slim fella realized he had a gift. So, what is yours?

This is good work. Have patience with all that remains unsolved in your heart. Let your inner teacher guide you.

Three minutes . . . thirty seconds . . . humble inquiry . . . gratitude. The questions get harder.

Question 4: How Does It Feel to Be a Problem?

I am not the first to pose this question. W. E. B. Du Bois penned this heart-wrenching question in his 1903 classic *The Souls of Black Folk*. How does it feel to be pedestal bound . . . alone in the world and told you are the measuring stick, the hope for ages past? How does it feel to be the scum of the earth . . . alone in the world and told you will never amount to much? How does it feel to be a problem? I asked this question to a group of youth in Hatchet Bay, Bahamas. Off the beaten path, Hatchet Bay was once a chicken plantation. Though the plantation had closed, the current residents were still equated with the filth and fetor of farm birds. These young people were told in school, "You ain't gone be nothing. . . . You'll end up just like your momma, your daddy, your uncle . . . 'cause you're from Hatchet Bay." Still, when posed this question, one wide-eyed preteen responded, "My mother works late. So I have to feed my younger siblings. I help them with homework. I tuck them in at night. I'm not a problem. I'm a problem solver." When you own your problem status, you develop a capacity of empathy for others, even if their problems are different than yours. Have you ever been a problem? How does it feel?

You may be a retired wealthy white man or young Hispanic woman trailblazing a path. Have you felt this way? I don't know your pain, but your inner teacher feels it. Seek a circle of trust and share your truth. Compassion and empathy await.

Three minutes . . . thirty seconds . . . humble inquiry . . . gratitude.

The questions get harder. If "Who am I?" is a question of identity, then "Why am I here?" is question of purpose. If "What is my gift?" is a question of vocation, then "How does it feel to be a problem?" is a question of resilience. Our final question is one of legacy.

Question 5: What Must I Do to Die a Good Death?

These words come from the interplanetary theologian Howard Washington Thurman. A good death? If you're a gang leader, is a good death your face on a T-shirt and a colored bandanna in a coffin? If you're a corporate executive, is a good death transferring multiple commas to the bank account of kids you never tucked in at night? Oh, how we fear the end . . . but a good death is predicated on a good life.

I took my children to an organizing meeting with a group of student activists. My headphoned tikes watched YouTube while we strategized. After the meeting, the students returned to the picket lines. As my kids and I walked to the car, a successive cycle of humble inquiries unfurled. "Why are they protesting?" asked my seven-year-old namesake. Unable to mince words and dilute the social unrest he felt in his heart, I explained, "Some police killed a black man for selling loose cigarettes. The police did not go to jail." Against the night sky, silence fell over my brown-faced boy. Then, penetrating the quiet, I heard, "Daddy, am I next?" Searching my soul for a sufficient reply, I responded, "Son, your mother and I work hard to protect you; we pray for you." "Daddy, I don't want you to be great . . . because they kill great people . . . and I want you to be my daddy." For my babies, I want to live a good life and die a good death. What must you do to die a good death?

Let deep speak unto deep, so that the love below might rise.

Three minutes . . . thirty seconds . . . humble inquiry . . . gratitude.

Share some love with your neighbor.

Every time we animate the Five Hard Questions, strangers who have never met share tears and embrace. For a passing moment, unlikely partners experience neighborly love. But in the euphoria of climbing out of the crevasse, I challenge these newfound neighbors to pose the Five Hard Questions collectively: Who are *we*? Why are *we* here? What is *our* gift? How does it feel to be a problem? What must *we* do to die a good death?

Both individually and collectively these hard questions constantly cycle through the depths of my soul. They call me and Fearless Dialogues to reckon with identity, purpose, vocation, resilience, and legacy. They challenge me and challenge us to lay aside insecurities and fears of appearing ignorant, in order to embrace the journey of not knowing. These questions remind me and remind us that, if we are humble enough to listen, inner teachers will show up in the unlikeliest of places: down in subways and over in Hatchet Bay, down in basement classrooms and over stone-ground grits, down in Florida's testosterone-filled room and in earshot of protest with a brown-faced boy. In the three-feet orbit of inner teachers, worlds are changed.

A FINAL WORD
A PRAYER

"If I go up to the heavens, you are there.
If I lie down in the deepest parts of the earth, you are also there."[49]
I give thanks that over a dozen years ago
You were down there . . . with us in the deep parts of the earth.

You were down there . . .
on that Underground Railroad when the professor freely spoke his
     truth.
You were down there . . .
when eyes drifted from the ceiling, my fiancé questioned, and I
     lifted the bill.
You were down there . . .
when I raised my downcast eyes and he looked lovingly into my
     pupils.
You were down there . . .
in the quiet, when
space lessened,
time froze, and
strangers became kin.
You were down there . . . in proximity to us.
Inviting inner teachers
to guide, to comfort,
to listen empathically,
and to inquire humbly.

Move us, dear God, so that deep might speak unto deep.
Compel us to face life's hardest questions in
our homes,
our community,
our country,
our world: Who are *we*?
             Why are *we* here?
             What is *our* gift?
             How does it feel to be a problem?
             What must *we* do to die a good death?

In the waiting moment, as truths rise from the deep,
we ask your blessing upon us, gracious God of silent tears.
For you are the one who can make a single teardrop from a litany
     of thank-yous

seep to the deepest parts of the earth and offer life-giving water to
    thirsting souls.
For wise instruction of subway professors, inner teachers, and your
    Holy Spirit
we give thanks
and ask it all
in your name.
Amen.

6

To Die a Good Death

Beyond the Fear
of Oppressive Systems

And there I stood. With my back against the wall and head on swivel, I scanned the lunchroom in search of the Big Three. Outsized and friendless, mere survival patterned the third day. Though my stomach grumbled, the fear in my heart prevented me from unlatching my lunch pail for the midday meal. Hunger was the least of my worries, for I spotted the Big Three towering over my classmates and knifing through the sea of newcomers; their eyes targeted me. This third day would be different. Determined not to give up my prized commodity, I clenched my fists and took a long deep breath . . .

At five, I carried no billfold or greenbacks. Nilla wafers were my kindergarten currency. These disc-shaped golden brown confections floated atop the cloud-like meringue of Momma's 'nana puddin'. Days after the 'nana puddin' vanished, Dad and I watched basketball on the wooden, floor-model tube and divvied up the reject wafers that were too broken to beautify Momma's meringue. Grandma loved Nilla wafers too. On hot summer days, we'd dip these sweet treats in tin cups of ice cold milk. After the plunge, the once-hardened milk-dipped exterior of the cookies dissolved in our mouths, creating a sugary sanctuary for our taste buds. Far more than cookies, Nilla wafers were priceless reminders of home. But on my first two days of kindergarten, three bullies stole my precious currency and my peace of mind.

So, as the Big Three approached on the third day, I sucked air into my lungs like woodwinds eyeing a conductor's baton and readied myself for confrontation. But, before the disharmonious conflict unfolded, a gentle giant placed his body between me and the Big Three. Interrupting the two-day ritual of bullying, the gentle giant asserted, "This is my cousin. You not gonna take his cookies anymore." The biggest behemoth eyed me once more, and without a single word he turned his back, and the other two mammoths followed him back into the sea.

With an outstretched hand, the gentle giant introduced himself, "I'm Brandon Williams." From that moment forward, Brandon became the watermark for which my life betides. He excelled in the classroom; I sought to follow his lead. Gregarious and fun loving, I patterned my friendships from his example. Come high school, we shared the blacktop, and my jump shot complemented his adept court vision. As teenagers, we stood shoulder to shoulder, but Brandon remained a giant in my eyes. And he taught me when giants fall, the ground quakes.

Some called it the game of the year. Nearly two thousand people squeezed onto Frederick Douglass High School's old wooden bleachers as we defended home court against our crosstown rival Benjamin E. Mays. In the jam-packed gymnasium, tensions were high and supportive fans erupted with cheers after every basket. Suddenly there was a scuffle in the bleachers, and the game briefly paused as police escorted a half-dozen students out of the gym. From a distance, one of the young men ushered out resembled Brandon. The game continued. I don't recall who won. But I will never forget the phone call late that evening.

It turns out Brandon was in the throng marshaled out of the gymnasium. The tussle that started at the ball game continued at the local hot-wing joint after the final buzzer sounded. As he had done for me a dozen years earlier, Brandon placed his body between the opposing factions. This time the mammoths did not turn away. Blindsided by an errant punch, Brandon hit the ground. Then bullets fatally pierced his flesh.

For months on end, my once-cherished Nilla wafers had an unsavory aftertaste of metal. Stomaching just one of the disc-shaped golden brown confections felt like swallowing a metric ton. Bound by the tragic demise of the gentle giant, life took on shades of flavorless grey, and no hopeful tunes filled my heart. Such was the lot of many of my friends. They too tasted metal and knew the sorrow songs.

Our chains are in the keep of the Keeper
in a labeled cabinet
on the second shelf by the cookies . . .
There's a rattle, sometimes.
You do not hear it who mind only
cookies and crunch them.
You do not hear the remarkable music— 'A
Death Song For You Before You Die.'
If you could hear it
you would make music too.[1]

(. . . shhh . . .)

For years, silence, not music, filled my heart. Over time, I gained the courage to penetrate the quietude and tell Brandon's story as an ode to a life well lived. With tear-filled eyes, I shared of our friendship in the company of Familiar Strangers, and I came to recognize his example as justice-bearing, sacrificial, and Christlike, in his advocacy for those with their head on swivel and backed against the wall. However, as many times as I have told of his boldness before students and unlikely partners around the world, I found myself ill-prepared to put his narrative to print.

I penned the first few pages of this chapter in mid-December. Every subsequent day in December, I returned to my desk to write, but no words would come. For more than three weeks, I found myself cemented in a writer's block and reliving the silent, music-less region of my heart.

In the sovereignty of those three weeks of quiet, I came to view Brandon and his interventionist strategies for peace metaphorically. Before the blank page, I reflected on behemoth-like oppressive systems that utilize institutional powers to shape language, inform actions, and create norms that signify who and what may be deemed desirable, acceptable, and normal. Then I turned my thoughts to the perception of larger-than-life systems that tower over the outsized and appear to function as impersonal dispassionate machines. Staring at the white space, I felt the rage and heard the silent tears of cornered individuals and communities who hunger for support and stand readied to fight for survival. In the eyes of the cornered, I recognized an existential weariness that I felt in my bones. In that achiness of spirit I realized that, regardless of the oppressive systems' shape, size, or form (e.g., political, educational, economic, family), systems that misappropriate power can destabilize the cornered by imperiling hope. I came to see these mammoth-sized threats to hope as the Big Three: despair, apathy, and shame. Once any or all of these three perilous threats seep into the hearts of those with their backs against the wall, resisting the unjust system becomes a more daunting challenge.

By thinking metaphorically, I came to see Brandon's life anew. To interrupt the Big Three, he placed his body between the towers and the outsized. While his conciliation immediately infused my life with hope, it cannot be understated that such an intervention placed him squarely in harm's way.

During my twenty-plus days of quiet contemplation, my soul wrestled with this metaphor and how it continues to influence my vocation, my theory of hope, and my understanding of Fearless Dialogues' approach to social change. In the writer's lull, to deepen my discernment, I sought wisdom in Scripture and in the works of Howard Thurman, Martin Luther, Luther Smith, and Donald Capps. In the presence of these master teachers, and the accompaniment of quiet, I heard the rhythmic sound of my breath.

(. . . shhh . . . listen . . .)

I could hear a melody of respiration that satisfied a deep hunger no sugared treat could fill. The tune was simple: "The Kingdom of God is within."[2] In true verse I learned that no keeper, even the rattling chains of death, could mute the sound of hope resonating from the chambers of the heart.

As a living symbol of Christ, Brandon's animating spirit struck a chord deep in my soul. A perfect synthesis of vocation, hope, and social change, his life and death were of equal importance, for they were of "a single respiration."[3] An inspiration to many, Brandon lived a courageous and full life. Likewise, his expiration, albeit tragic, was equally bold and impactful. A good life begat a good death. Since that fated evening in the winter of 1994, Brandon's single respiration of life and death has invigorated me to use my finitely numbered breaths to strategically interrupt oppressive systems through Fearless Dialogues.

History has shown that a good life and a good death can interrupt the stranglehold of malevolent individual and institutional goliaths. In this final chapter, we wrestle with the dominant metaphor of Brandon's life and death as a pathway to examine vocations of resistance, theories of hope, and the strategies utilized by Fearless Dialogues to resist oppressive systems. But first, a few words of direction for you, Beloved Reader.

In drafting this chapter, I faced long, sacred silences in the shadow regions of my heart. While traversing the luminous darkness, trusted companions raised probing questions about vision, faith, and mortality.[4] Their queries were pillars of fire to guide me through the dark caverns of my soul. Recognizing how much I learned in the beautiful struggle of facing these ultimate realities, in this chapter I offer you a similar opportunity to have a fearless dialogue with yourself.

In the succeeding pages, it is my hope that the accounts revealed and theories examined serve as a mirror for you. As you recall your mammoths, face the Big Three, and reflect on the gentle giants who intervened on your behalf, I beckon you to welcome the sacred silence as a site for learning and gratitude. Likewise, these accounts may serve as triggers that catalyze a reassessment of call, a reclaiming of hope, and a renewed fervor to serve. For these reasons, I stand in the stead of my trusted companions and pose probing questions to stimulate your discovery. To alter the pace of your reading and offer pause for deeper deliberation, I italicize these questions. I pray that on this journey into the contemplative quiet, you hear the pitch-perfect sound of vocation, and the deeper notes of hope. It is this music from within that will stave off our justice fatigue and compel us to interrupt oppressive systems in this life, so that we too may die a good death.

THE PICTURE OF AN ACTIVIST?: QUESTIONING VOCATION, DISTORTING SELF

The volcano erupts when it wills. Its lava clears a path. In the wake of its destruction, new life must start afresh.

After graduate school, I pitched my vocational tent on a volatile hotspot. Above the surface, I presented as a young, confident, and finely dressed tenure-track professor with an ability to care through teaching, preaching, and advocacy. Beneath the surface, the ground tremored and small explosions of self-doubt created fissures in my vocational outlook: *What good is a behind-the-scenes public intellectual? How can I be a prophetic preacher without a pulpit to proclaim? Can I call myself an activist, if I rarely find a picket line?* The spouting steam, the smell of ash, the thundering rumbles from within should have been ample warning.

Yet I was ill-prepared for the vocational eruption one year and one day after the tragic death of Michael Brown. From my home in

Atlanta, I kept a close eye on the social unrest still simmering in Ferguson, Missouri. On the first week of August 2015, scores of old friends, colleagues, and mentors flocked to the Show-Me state. From afar, I read about the panels, think tanks, and rallies, all organized to memorialize Michael Brown, protest police brutality, and call America to reckon with its history of systemic racism. Through social media and national news outlets, I tracked close friends protesting and standing alongside the fearless young adults spearheading the Black Lives Matter movement.

On that Monday afternoon, I felt a deep burning on the inside as I digitally followed the footsteps of the three hundred protestors marching from Christ Church Cathedral to Missouri's Thomas Eagleton federal courthouse. Around 1:30 p.m. my magma boiled as nearly a quarter of those chanting protestors crossed the barricade surrounding the courthouse. Face to face with giants in police gear and bulletproof vests, the unarmed protestors interlocked their arms and as a human chain readied themselves for conflict. Detainment was expected.

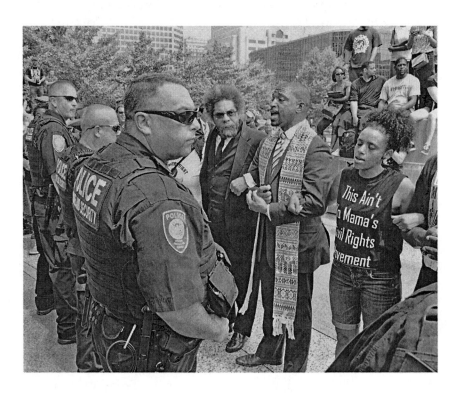

However, I did not anticipate the hot molten lava that scorched my spirit and leveled my sense of vocation when I saw "the picture" scroll across my Facebook wall.

In "the picture," my teacher, my old friend, and my little sister stood arm in arm before vested officers. As Facebook commentators "liked" "the picture" and pronounced their opinions, my eyes watered and steaming lava spouted from the screen. Inflamed by feelings of guilt, hypocrisy, and vocational unrest, I closed my laptop. Storming questions cleared a path that leveled my self-understanding as a scholar, minister, and activist: *Where am I? Why am I here? Why am I not there? Who am I?* Hours upon hours, day after day, I gazed at "the picture," and in the wake of the destruction one question remained: *Who am I not?*

From one angle, "the picture" spoke a thousand words about my educational formation, my ministerial calling, and my identity as an activist. Yet from another angle, it debunked my self-understanding as a public intellectual, a prophetic minister, and an activist on the front lines. Squarely at the intersection between "Who am I?" and "Who am I not?" this vocational crisis forced me into months of critical introspection and therapeutic intervention. Sifting through the devastation of my incinerated vocation, I searched for signs of hope, lessons for life.

Have you been there? What decisions have you made, or better yet, what decisions have been made for you that leveled your sense of purpose, your understanding of vocation? When all that you have worked for and all that you have built lies in ruin, how do you search for meaning? So . . . now what?

A fearless dialogue with my self proved mandatory. So I entered into a place of contemplative quiet, and I undertook the process of deconstructing "the picture" metaphorically. The pixelated image became a roadmap for my return to self and a compass to reclaim my calling. First, I examined the three whom I deemed the protagonists in "the picture": my teacher, my old friend, and my little sister. Then came an epiphany about the mammoths.

The Teacher

In the center of the image, donning his uniformed black suit and tie, stood my teacher, Cornel West, nationally recognized for his philosophical depth as a social critic, his quick wit before the media, and his love ethic that placed him on the side of the oppressed. I first met Dr. West in 2004 as a student in a doctoral seminar he cotaught at Princeton University titled, "An Introduction to African-American Intellectual Thought." During the course we discussed all manner of public intellectuals who spoke out against lynching, economic disparity, educational inequities, and white supremacy. In "the picture," West looks out beyond the photographer, and I imagined him questioning me: "Where do you fit in the lineage of African American intellectuals?" As I pondered who I was as a public intellectual, answers flowed: I am not Cornel West. I am not W. E. B. Du Bois, Booker T. Washington, Anna Julia Cooper, Toni Morrison, or James Baldwin. I am not, I am not, I am not.

The Clergy Friend

Standing by my teacher, like a tree planted by the water, was my sure-footed clergy friend, the Rev. Starsky Wilson. Rev. Starsky and I met in a sleepy suburb of St. Louis during his final year of seminary. Even then, he articulated a prophetic vision for a community undivided by race, educational disparities, and class. I was privy to his dreams long before he was named CEO of the Deaconess Foundation, appointed by the Missouri governor as cochair of the Ferguson Commission, or chosen to serve as senior pastor of St. John's United Church of Christ. Then, on August 9, 2014, Michael Brown was shot, eleven miles from his office at the Deaconess Foundation and fourteen miles from the church he pastored. As the foment of Ferguson's discontent began to mirror the Montgomery and Selma of old, a small cadre of prophetic leaders like Rev. Starsky began to emerge. By day, he leveraged his resources as a philanthropist and worked with select members of the faith community to offer sanctuary for persons seeking refuge. By night, he weathered intemperate climates and literally stood behind dozens of young activists and prayed as they chanted, "Why are you in riot gear? We don't see no riot here!" Day after day I stared at "the picture," and in the eyes of my beloved friend I saw the best of the prophetic preaching tradition. Still, I could not help but ask, "Who am I?" I am not Starsky Wilson. I am not Martin Luther King, Adam Clayton Powell, Traci Blackmon, Teresa Fry Brown, or Gardner C. Taylor. I am not, I am not, I am not.

The Activist Sister

I'm still unsure which was more shocking, seeing my little sister standing before armed police or digesting the declarative statement on her sleeveless shirt, "This Ain't Yo Mama's Civil Rights Movement." While Rahiel Tesfamariam is not my biological sibling, within hours of meeting we knew we were kin. As I trekked through my doctoral program at Princeton Theological Seminary, Rahiel found her wings as a graduate student and international ambassador for justice at Yale Divinity School. Always a crystal-clear writer, with the ability to pull on the heartstrings and convict the spirit of her readership, it was no surprise that after graduation Rahiel started an online magazine on faith and culture, and eventually became a columnist for the *Washington Post*. Because of her history as an organizer in California and Washington, DC, she emerged as a central figure in articulating the positions of a new millennium of activists unbound by the respectability politics of old. Like Angela Davis, Assata Shakur, Stokely Carmichael, Darnell Moore, and countless members of the Black Lives Matter movement, there stood my sister steadfast and unswayed. Yet I am neither Rahiel Tesfamariam nor the previously named political activists. These I am not.

The Mammoths

"The picture" tormented me because I did not fit within my idealized vision of scholar, minister, or activist. One day I noticed the mammoths, and the metaphor deepened. Each of the vested officers standing before my teacher, friend, and sister donned black sunglasses. Two ideas percolated.

1. Shielded eyes inhibit access to the soul. Coupled with a state-issued uniform, heavy artillery, and a dispassionate scowl, this thin opaque glass barrier walled off human connection with the officers. It further made the individuals who took oaths to protect and serve appear more like giant militaristic machines. *How does one resist the hope-impairing tendency to depersonalize systems and dehumanize people as part of a larger machine? What might we gain by seeing the particular individual who is associated with a larger system?*

2. Sunglasses also cast reflections like distorting mirrors. While face-to-face with the officers, a glance into the opaque shades would reveal

a smaller version of the self. When we stand before our giants, the reflection of ourselves appears diminished, our ability to create change may seem infinitesimal, and we may unconsciously cling to a vocation of negation, that we are not enough. *While not diminishing the impact of die-ins, sit-ins, and marches, might we conceive of activism more expansively? How do we thwart distortions of smallness by living into vocations of resistance that do not fit neatly within the parameters of pictured activism?*

The symbolism of "the picture" served as an inner labyrinth for me to spiral to the center of my vocational core. Inside of me, the teacher, the minister, the activist stood side by side, but few opportunities existed to fuse the gifts of these roles. At times, my lectures felt a bit preachy, my sermons sounded professorial, and my advocacy emanated from my faith; but rare was the space to integrate the three. In the chance opportunities when the three vocational identities took on a singular voice, on one hand, I felt the wholesome peace of an internal resolve. On the other hand, I felt the external discomfort of a punitive gaze from other teachers, ministers, and activists, because my hybrid approach to service was far too different from the norm. *If social change is the ultimate aim, and vocational wholeness is the goal, why should I care if I am looked at askance?*

Perhaps you have felt this inner division and outer tumult in seeking to integrate your passions and your work. Yet I wonder, how can we stand before mammoths like race, class, and homophobia and effectuate change if we are divided from within and castigated for serving differently? For answers, I suggest we look into the shaded eyes of our mammoths. In the dark reflecting glass, we can see our insecurities around vocational fit, and examine how a litany of *I am nots* flattens our ability to create change.

THE PROBLEMS OF FIT, THE PERILS OF FLAT: BEYOND A VOCATION OF NEGATION

For months on end, I scrutinized "the picture" and defined my vocation through a process of negation. *I am not* a public intellectual in the form of Cornel West. *I am not* functioning in the prophetic preaching tradition in the same fashion as the Rev. Starsky Wilson. *I am not* standing on the frontlines or crafting overtly politicized publications like my activist-oriented sister Rahiel Tesfamariam. Haunted by *I am nots*, I lost any semblance of certainty around my call, and the questions returned: *If I'm clear on who I am not, then who am I? Are there ways to live out my calling that don't amplify my difference? Why do I care so much about how others perceive my service?* Bedeviled by my vocation of negation, more than ever I wrestled with the problem of "fit."

Discerning vocational fit may sometimes come with intense struggle. Such can be said of the Protestant reformer Martin Luther. In the psychobiography *Young Man Luther*, Erik Erikson examines a period of identity crisis in Martin Luther's life that has been contested by generations of scholars. Erikson chronicles that at the age of twenty-three and in the throes of vocational discernment, Martin Luther experienced an epileptic fit while singing in the monastery choir where he trained for the priesthood. As Martin Luther fell to the floor, he cried out, "I am not! I am not!" Erikson argues that this declaration of negation has at least two interpretations. During the Middle Ages such a psychosomatic eruption may have been interpreted as demonic. Therefore, in his fall to the ground, young man Luther may have been decrying "I am not . . . possessed."[5] Another interpretation is more vocational in nature and aligns with the metaphor of seeing the reflection of oneself in the face of a giant.

Before Luther entered the monastery, his father subjected him to years of strict schooling, with hopes that his son would enter politics or administration. However, at the age of twenty-one, without his father's permission, Martin Luther abruptly left the University of Erfurt, where he was slated to study law, and decided to enter the monastery. Therefore, his fit in the choir may have been a protest against his lack of vocational "fit" in the legal community. Perhaps, in his epileptic fall, prior to blacking out, young man Luther saw himself in the face of the giant patriarch and cried out, "I am not . . . what my father said I was."[6]

Through Martin Luther's lens, "I am not" is not a diminishment of commitment, but a differentiation of call. By declaring that he was not the sum total of his father's hopes and dreams, Martin Luther demarcated himself from the expectations of how he should bring about change in the world. In a recent conversation with my dear friend and teacher Luther Smith, he echoed similar sentiments and advocated for an expansion of how we see vocations of activism and callings for social change:

> For some people, there is only a certain kind of activism that counts, and I think this is a sad thing. This type of thinking resides within many in the black community, but [this thinking also] gets imposed

on the black community such that the only folks worth really writing about in our history books are people like Martin Luther King or Thurgood Marshall. [If you look at only these] public figures, you lose so many black intellectuals that feed what it means to be a people and you lose the artists that shape awareness. [You also] lose the contributions of the folks that are really inspiring awareness and engagement in communities that will never have their name in the paper. It just *flattens* what it means to be an activist.[7]

A flattened view of activism not only neglects the efforts for communal change enacted by those who fall out of the spotlight. It also casts a shadow on alternative approaches to social change that do not fit within the expected parameters of front-line protests. Through media coverage, historical interpretations, and legal determinants, oppressive systems further flatten activism by normalizing some forms of protest as desirable and stigmatizing other forms of resistance as insurgent. For instance, a silent protest on the state capitol steps would likely be cast in a more favorable light than a die-in that obstructs the traffic of a state highway. To this end, the distorting mirrors of oppressive systems make the criterion for activism and social change too small to contain other vocational identities aligned with social action. Regretfully, far too many change agents succumb to these pressures by cramming themselves into the confines of desirable protest or insurgent resistance, in order to make their work recognizable.

For me, the matters of fitting and flatness extend beyond individual vocational identity. These concerns have organizational implications for how Fearless Dialogues is classified and does its work. By adopting the dominant approaches of neither the NAACP nor Black Lives Matter, does the work of Fearless Dialogues qualify as desirable protest or resistant insurgency? While not being aligned with an academic institute, does the work of Fearless Dialogues register as possessing the appropriate intellectual depth? Given its lack of denominational backing and its unwillingness to proselytize, does the faith-induced work of Fearless Dialogues fall short of God-centeredness? The confining limits of acceptable means to serve are tools of oppressive systems to asphyxiate vocational identity and strangle organizational creativity.

. . . so, breathe . . .

The Good News is that the creative force of change can never be bound by flattening norms and stifling stigmas. For just a moment, let us consider embracing forms of social action that exist beyond the picket lines. *How does your work in the hospital, the church, the large corporation, the fast-food chain, or within your family afford you opportunities to share knowledge, engage spirit, and advocate for others? How might we recast our perspectives of activist-oriented service and our vocational outlooks on social change?*

The more I reflected on "the picture," Martin Luther's seizure, and Luther Smith's sage words on flatness, the more I recognized how desperately I sought to retrofit my square vocational peg into a circular hole that would validate my call. Even with worldly validations like promotion and tenure, peer-reviewed publications, preaching opportunities, and partnerships with communities, my vocational peg still felt unshapely. Moving beyond a vocation of negation requires seeking not to fit or flatten one's life work into a truncated label or neat category like scholar, minister, or activist. To the contrary, a more artistic approach to vocation proves necessary. Seeking inspiration from artistry, I sought the guidance of a master artisan to help me carve my unshapely vocational peg into a sculpture that seamlessly integrated the creative mind, the mystical spirit, and the heart to care *with* the unacknowledged.

Like a wide-eyed apprentice, I watched this master navigate nimbly around reductionist categories of how he should serve. I took notice of his inventive intellect, boundless depth of spirit, and unencumbered sense of advocacy. The more I turned to this craftsman, the more I recognized a way forward for advocates like me who do not fit flat descriptions of activism. So too did I observe his organizational craftiness in carving out spaces for unlikely partners to engage in heartfelt conversation with self, other, and the surrounding world. Lastly, and perhaps most importantly, I examined how this master artisan utilized an interrupting hope to place himself between the Big Three and the outsized who found their backs against the wall. Let us learn from the wisdom of yet another gentle giant who forged his own vocational path, carried hope for the disinherited, and, ultimately, died a good death: the Rev. Howard Washington Thurman.

THE GENTLE GIANT AND THE BIG THREE: AN INTERRUPTING HOPE IN THE FACE OF SYSTEMIC THREATS

Born forty-four days before the turn of the twentieth century, Howard Washington Thurman was raised in the segregated town of Daytona,

Florida. Reared by a widowed mother with few financial means, from an outsider's view, upward mobility for young man Howard seemed bleak. But his grandmother Nancy Ambrose, who was born a slave, "did not allow him to accept the educational limitations placed on black youth in their community."[8] Spurred by a need to assist his family, a hope from ages past, and a commitment to personal growth, young Thurman became the first African American youth in Daytona to receive an eighth-grade certificate from the public schools.[9] Need I mention that while completing this feat, he also worked full-time at a fish market? Though he completed eighth grade with a 99 percent grade point average, his thirst for knowledge remained unquenched.[10]

In the early 1900s, only three public high schools existed for African American youth in the state of Florida, but there were several private, church-supported high schools in the region that accepted African American students. Mother Thurman offered her son a good-will blessing to pursue his education, but with only a meager income to support the rearing of his sisters, she could provide no monetary assistance in support of his dreams. With the little money he had saved, Thurman applied and was accepted at the Florida Baptist Academy of Jacksonville.

When the time came to leave Daytona and continue his education in Jacksonville, young man Howard left for the railway and purchased a train ticket. But he could not afford to ship his few belongings, packed away in an old ramshackle trunk. Overtaken by despair, Thurman sat down on the steps of the railway station, dropped his head, and cried his young heart out. Moments later, he opened his tear-filled eyes; standing before him was a large black man in overalls donning a denim cap. "Boy, what in the hell are you crying about?" the gentle giant questioned. The adolescent Thurman explained his predicament. After hearing the young lad's quandary, the man in overalls replied, "If you're trying to get out of this damn town to get an education, the least I can do is to help you." Moments later, the gentle giant pulled out his rawhide money bag, and paid for the delivery of young Howard's baggage. "Then, without a word, he turned and disappeared down the railroad track." The two would never meet again.[11] *Who are the people, whose names we'll never know, who sacrificed for our hopes and found value in our vocation?*

In Howard Thurman's earliest surviving correspondence to Mordecai Wyatt Johnson, he described in a letter of introduction to his soon-to-be mentor the hardships faced during his days of high school and his vocational quest to serve the needs of his people. After perfunctory words of salutation, the eighteen-year-old Thurman opened the missive with these words, "Listen while I tell to you my soul." He revealed that in his first year of high school, he had no money, had insufficient winter clothing, and ate an average of one square meal a day. To make ends meet, he pressed clothes in the community and worked a thirteen-hour shift on Saturdays. In spite of his dire straits, he finished his first year with a 96 percent grade point average, the highest in the school. In his second and third year at the school, he earned a 98 percent and a 94 percent respectively. From his written testimony, the reader clearly grasps young man Howard's insatiable quest to learn.[12]

In the oldest surviving letter of Thurman's voluminous papers, he expresses a weariness around vocational fit and a discontent with a flat view of service. This problem of fit and peril of flatness would echo throughout his writings, lectures, and sermons for the remaining sixty-four years of his life. Hear these words of hopeful duress in the adolescent voice of young man Howard's letter to Johnson:

> I want to be a minister of the Gospel. I feel the needs of my people. I see their distressing conditions, and have offered myself upon the altar as a living sacrifice, in order that I may help the "skinned and flung down." . . . I am scheduled to finish here next year. As you know the war is on and young men are being snatched daily. I am patriotic, I am willing to fight for democracy, but my friend Rev. Johnson, my people need me.[13]

Like young man Luther, who was struck by a fit in a monastery choir nearly four centuries earlier, the adolescent Thurman was crying out before a different altar. He saw and felt the plight of his people and was willing to lay down his life on their behalf, but can't you hear young Thurman crying out, "I am not . . . a soldier"? He desired a life of service, but the parameters of contributing with mind, spirit, and action were confining and small.

Seeking guidance on how to integrate his love of learning, his spiritual longing, and his commitment to liberation, this vocationally disoriented adolescent concluded his letter with a prayer request: "Please pray for me because (almost) on every hand, I am discouraged in my choice of the Ministry. Sometimes I think nobody cares but thank God, Jesus does, mother does, and I believe you do."[14]

Hope was not lost in this young man, who at an early age was backed against the wall by poverty, educational disparities, and widespread racial discrimination. While the Big Three threats to hope—despair, apathy, and shame—lingered near, he continued to push forward in the classroom and on the job. Yet, as his first letter concludes, we hear the eighteen-year-old crying out desperately and searching with head on swivel for a community of reliable others to sustain his hope, support his educational aspirations, and affirm his call. Given the odds stacked against him, questions abounded regarding his next steps.

Faced with daily deprivation, where did young man Thurman find hope to complete high school as the valedictorian of his class? How did he overcome *despair* during his student years at Morehouse College, where he read every book in the library and graduated as valedictorian? Where did he gain the fortitude to contest *apathy* in the Ku Klux Klan–ridden towns of western New York where he finished seminary and preached sermons before open-minded liberals and hard-hearted racists?[15] What disrupted *shame* from settling in Thurman's soul, when he worked in the impoverished communities surrounding the resource-rich institutions that paid his salary (Morehouse College, Spelman College, Howard University, Boston College, and the Church for the Fellowship of All Peoples) as professor, dean, and pastor?

I am certain he found a fundament of hope in an eclectic community of reliable others. Maybe in the thoughtful words and prodigious example of teachers and mentors like Mary McLeod Bethune, Mordecai Wyatt Johnson, and Benjamin Mays, he tapped into a wisdom to confront despair. Quite possibly, his otherworldly conversations with Gandhi, Rufus Jones, foreign travelers, little children, the Atlantic Ocean, and an old oak tree placed him in a spiritual realm to contest the whims of apathy. Certainly reading the Bible to his illiterate grandmother, Nancy Ambrose, welcomed the presence of God and boundary-breaking teachings of Jesus in his life to stymie shame, ground his ego, and safeguard him from a superiority complex.

The timing must have been providential. Back in 2014, Westminster John Knox Press endowed me with the task of writing this book. Under tenure review that same year, I accepted the unenviable task of compiling a 600-page dossier for others to assess my publications, my teaching, and my service to the church and the world. Far heavier than the twenty-pound document was the burdensome yoke of not fitting into the prototypical mold of professor, pastor, and activist. Feeling that I was under constant review by colleagues with access to 600 pages of my life, I walked the corridors of Emory University with head on swivel.

Questioning self, scholarship, and service, and with my back against the wall, I felt a towering presence drawing near. It was intent on taking my most precious commodity, hope. Wearied from the mounting pressures, I still readied myself for the fight. But before the internal conflict imploded, Thurman's body of work stood between me and the Big Three (despair, apathy, and shame).

For the past three years, especially during my travails in facing "the picture," Howard Thurman has journeyed with me as a reliable other. In this time, not only have his life and work shifted my understanding of vocations of resistance; his canon has also helped to refine my theory of hope, which is central to the work of Fearless Dialogues. Hereafter, I share with you how the impress of Thurman's corpus has contributed to this evolution of thought and action.

JESUS, THE DISINHERITED, AND A WILDERNESS CONFRONTATION WITH THE BIG THREE: CHARTING PATHS OF RESISTANCE AND NONRESISTANCE

What do the life and teachings of Jesus say to those who stand with their backs against the wall? This question was never impersonal for Thurman, as one raised in a Christian nation with a sordid history of slavery, lynching, and segregation. In 1935, during a pilgrimage of friendship to India, Thurman was forced to articulate how he could justify vocationally positioning himself as an agent of hope in a Christian tradition that exploited persons of color.

One day, following a lecture at the University of Colombo in Sri Lanka,[16] Thurman received a soul-shifting challenge by a Hindu administrator. Though the administrator knew the stated purpose of Thurman's visit was a pilgrimage of friendship, he could not fathom how an intelligent African American man could speak so affirmatively of a Christianity that inflicts harm on people of color. With no reservation, the administrator tendered a tremulous question, "What are *you* doing here?" To contextualize his question, he reminded Thurman of how his African forebears were forced into bondage by Christian slaveholders. He then cited accounts of Christian ministers who used religion and scriptural passages from the apostle Paul to sanction the system of slavery. The host even mentioned a newspaper article reporting an all-white Christian church interrupting Sunday worship to join a lynch mob. The Hindu host wondered aloud how Thurman could claim the same Christian tradition utilized to impose political segregation, social isolation, and economic inequality on his own people. After listing this diatribe of ills, the administrator crudely invited Thurman to conversation by calling him "a traitor to all the darker peoples of the earth."[17] That afternoon, Thurman and the Hindu administrator engaged in five hours of fearless dialogues about Thurman's commitment to the religion of Jesus.

More than a decade after the five-hour conversation, Thurman published a small but important book titled *Jesus and the Disinherited*. A bold social application of Thurman's biblical interpretation, the book undermines religious justification for segregation, asserts the worth of the underprivileged, and confronts structures complicit with injustice.[18] In order to make the case that the underprivileged have direct access to God, Thurman locates Jesus as one of the disinherited in his age. This interpretative lens provides the reader with a unique angle to examine Jesus' unconventional approach to contesting oppressive systems. However, if we take one step backward, the book also offers a glimpse of how Thurman vocationally positioned himself to engage in a life of activism beyond snug categorization. So let us look closer at how young man Jesus, and Thurman, uncovered a path of resistance beyond the conventional bounds of activism and social change.

Thurman makes three incisive conclusions that situated young man Jesus as one among many disinherited of his age.[19] Each of the following conditions in Jesus' life placed him in an unavoidable position of discerning how he would face a system that abused him and those he loved:

1. Jesus was a Jew. According to Thurman, "it is impossible for Jesus to be understood outside of the sense of community which Israel held with God."[20] Jesus of Nazareth's Judaic origin is not coincidental but central and cannot be severed from the Christian tradition. Jesus went about his Father's business as a Jew of Palestine.[21]

2. Jesus was poor. His family was so strapped that at birth his parents could afford only a dove, not the traditional lamb, as a sacrificial offering on his behalf. This suggests that, from birth, Jesus was linked with "the great mass of poor people on earth."[22]

3. Jesus was a member of a minority group in the midst of a larger, more dominant group. Prior to Jesus' birth, Palestine fell under Roman occupation. Taxes were increased. Temples honoring

the occupying state were raised on Israel's holy soil. Any element of insurgency was snuffed out with force. Therefore, as a poor Jew, Jesus was a minority raised in a climate where he was not afforded the protections and guarantees of Roman citizenship. "If a Roman soldier pushed Jesus into a ditch, he could not appeal to Caesar; he would be just another Jew in the ditch."[23]

Given these assertions about Jesus' origins, economic condition, and social status, Thurman posits that as a Jewish youth in Palestine, young man Jesus had to discern, "How will I reckon with Rome?" "This question was not academic. It was the most crucial of questions. In essence, Rome was the enemy; Rome symbolized total frustration; Rome was the great barrier to peace of mind. And Rome was everywhere. No Jewish person of the period could deal with the question of his practical life, his vocation, his place in society until he had settled deep within himself this critical issue."[24]

Not unlike young man Howard, who fell under the heavy yoke of segregation and white supremacy, young man Jesus was forced to question, "*What must be the attitude toward the rulers, the controllers of political, social, and economic life?*"[25] Thurman outlines that Jesus and other Jews in Palestine were faced with narrowly defined options of how they might respond to Rome's oppressive system: resist or not resist.

Nonresistance

In Thurman's purview, the path of nonresistance takes one of two forms. The first path leads to assimilation. Through patterns of imitation, the disinherited bow a knee to the powerful and yield qualities once held as germane to self as unworthy. Such submission diminishes self-respect and often requires shunning one's heritage, customs, and faith. Thurman argues that the Sadducees, who were high priests and the most economically stable of the Palestinian Jews, made public peace with Rome by becoming like them. While they loved Israel, this assimilation ensured their security and maintained their status.[26] *Like the Sadducees, have you given up or given in to oppressive systems for security and self-interests? If so, what have been the benefits? What have been the costs?*

The other path of nonresistance is cultural isolation. Recognizing that actively contesting a behemoth system is a daunting task for an outsized group, these nonresistant persons reduce contact with the oppressor to a minimum. While not actively resistant, these disinherited persons steeped in a rejected culture may very well harbor resentment, bitterness, hatred, and fear. Thurman connotes the Pharisees of Jesus' day, who did not actively resist Rome, but held a terrible contempt for them, might be classified as cultural isolationists.[27] *Like the Pharisees, have you sequestered yourself from oppressive systems and tempered your tongue to stave off further rejection and harm? If so, what have been the benefits? What have been the costs?*

Resistance

"Why can't something be done? We must do something!" cry the disinherited wearied by prolonged bully tactics. "By 'something' is meant action, direct action, as over against words, subtleties, threats, and innuendos."[28] Yet these calls for forceful action emerge as a last resort for the disinherited, because of an awareness that such resistance may lead to a tragic end. Once this mood is established, the overtly resistant determine it is better to die fighting for change than to live as quietly compliant. In its most radicalized form, overt resistance adopts a tragically flat view of activism, that those who choose not to take arms and fight display conformity, complicity, or cowardice. The Zealots of Jesus' day carried such beliefs. Undeterred by the consequence of death, they mobilized a small organized movement of forceful action to place pressure on the persecutory system. Recognizing this insatiable fervor for change, Jesus welcomed a Zealot into his band of twelve disciples. But he chose a different path. *Like the Zealots, have you chosen a path of overt resistance and in spite of your good intentions ostracized potential allies who choose to fight differently? If so, what have been the benefits? What have been the costs?*

We know little of Jesus' youth, but we know that he must have wrestled with these three self-limiting parameters of how to contest the Roman state. I surmise that at some point between his three-day lesson with the teachers in the temple courts at age twelve and his heaven-opening baptism years later, young man Jesus had a crisis of fit. Can you hear him calling out to the heavens, "I am not the Sadducees. I am not the Pharisees. I am not the Zealots. I am not, I am not, I am not"?

Young man Jesus must have recognized that a tool of oppressive systems is to pit the outsized against each other. He must have understood the perilous effects when disinherited persons direct their energy into fitting within narrowly framed categories of nonresistant or resistant. On his way to the temple at twelve, had he met the daughter of a Sadducee, who had neither succumbed to apathy nor accepted the assimilationist tendencies of her parents? Walking to meet John the Baptist at the lake, could he have swapped words with the son of a Pharisee, who staved off shame and did not yet harbor isolationist discontent? With fresh eyes after seeing the heavens opened, did he meet a teen from a Zealot household, with fire in his belly, who sought to fight the Roman state a different way?

With questions of how to live out a vocation of resistance vying for Jesus' attention, Thurman suggests that, shortly after his baptism, a more pressing question settled on Jesus' heart: "*What shall I do with my life if I am going to be true to the tremendous experience of God which I have had?*"[29] To carve out a more fulsome form of activism, the young carpenter found a place of complete and utter isolation where he could engage in a fearless dialogue with self . . . the desert.

A Wilderness Confrontation with the Big Three

Scripture tells us that in the wilderness Jesus faced three temptations. Upon closer examination, these temptations parallel the Big Three threats to hope (despair, apathy, and shame) and are representative of the models of nonresistance and resistance that Jesus saw in his youth.

Only days into the wilderness, as Jesus yearns for a meal, a malevolent voice beckons to an empty-stomached Jesus, "If you are the Son of God, tell these stones to become bread." This parasitic thought of apathy[30] challenges Jesus to stop resisting hunger and to eat now, because a future meal is too far away. Likely lethargic and longing for food, Jesus understands that to eat bread during a period of fasting will sever the sacrificial connection required for spiritual discernment. In a famished state, perhaps he reasons that this first temptation of hunger is synonymous with the desire of the Sadducees to prioritize their material well-being over psychological and spiritual wholeness. Therefore, he speaks back to the malevolent voice, "Humans do not live on bread alone." While bread is necessary for physical survival, neglecting the hungers of the mind and spirit leaves one psychologically empty, spiritually mal-nourished, and ill-prepared to fight for social change.

Even more wearied from the pilgrimage journey, Jesus finds him-self atop a high cliff when the malevolent voice returns: "If you are the Son of God, throw yourself down." The tempter is saying to Jesus that the world is not orderly or structured, so control what you can: yourself. "There is no fundamental dependability upon which you can depend. But if you can get into a certain position of immunity, then the ordinary logic of life can be handled and manipulated."[31] Did not the Pharisees, through isolation, seek a form of immunity to control self and shun all else? Jesus understood that physical isolation does not immunize one from the psychospiritual ills of bitterness and shame. To move in the world with a diminished sense of self and a belief that one is internally flawed is to live life on the edge of a high cliff. In Jesus' response, "Do not put the Lord your God to the test," he contests internal forces of self-doubt that can snuff out his life before his minis-try of resistance unfolds.

Near the end of his forty-day pilgrimage in the wilderness, Jesus finds himself at another high place overlooking the splendorous king-doms of the world. Then a final word from the tempter: "All this I will give you, if you will bow down and worship me." The final temptation of power proves no less difficult to overcome. Jesus is surrounded by people under the press of despair, whose futures seem blocked by the oppressive regime of Rome. As a poor Jew from an underprivileged minority group, young man Jesus feels the needs of his people and is willing to lay himself on the altar for the skinned and flung down. Looking down upon the kingdom, a tempting quest for power and an impatience for change lie at his fingertips. Maybe Jesus considers the following: If I accept the tempter's final offer, I can land a strate-gic position, like governor of Palestine, and work within the political systems to better the lot of my people. Or I can rally the Zealots and antiestablishment insurgents to organize a movement to overthrow the empire by force. The historically adept Jesus knows the substantive kingdom-building works of his politically savvy forebears Joseph and David. He also cannot dismiss the militant passions of the Zealots. Resistance through political action and direct force are in view. Yet these options of resistance run counter to Jesus' life course: "Away from me, Satan!" Blazing a trail out of the wilderness, Jesus uncovers another way to resist, which starts from within.

I AM, THE WAY BEYOND FIT AND FLAT:
FIVE FEAR+LESS ALTERNATIVE PATHS OF RESISTANCE

I Am the Way

Upon exiting the desert, all of the sand, rocks, and high cliffs had new meaning for young man Jesus. In the vast openness of the wilderness, his face-off with the Big Three tempters clarified that his path to contesting Rome would not take the form of assimilation or isolation, or be limited to direct action. Before him lay a seemingly endless road from head to heart. So, in an intemperate social climate that denied him full citizenship, dehumanized the disinherited, and left a narrow margin for contesting oppression, Jesus set in motion a vocation of resistance that would be revered, studied, and duplicated the world over.

Far from assimilationist, Jesus laid a path to social change that placed him in constant contact with unlikely partners. He dined with tax collectors and sinners[32] and touched lepers defiled as unclean.[33] He sipped water with a Samaritan woman[34] and came to the aid of a Roman soldier, though both were detested by Jesus' people.[35] In the company of unlikely partners, he taught and learned, healed and liberated.

Neither did Jesus live a life of withdrawal. To the contrary, he engaged in heartfelt conversation on taboo subjects. Standing in earshot of Pharisees, Jesus healed a man in the synagogue, and then explained why he broke the religious law to do so on the Sabbath.[36] So too Jesus placed his body between a woman caught in adultery and a crowd of Pharisees intent on stoning her for breaking Moses' law. In a master class on interruption, Jesus stooped to his knees, wrote in the sand, and spoke back to her accusers, "All right, but let the one who has never sinned throw the first stone!"[37]

Though he never took up arms, time and time again Jesus altered spaces by directly confronting dissenters. To reclaim the sanctity and sacredness of the worship space, Jesus turned over tables and drove out money changers who set up shop in the temple courts.[38] On the day of his arrest, an unarmed Jesus placed his body between the disciples he loved and a band of soldiers who carried torches, lanterns, and weapons. Preventing a melee, he stood directly before his accusers and stated, "If you are looking for me, then let these men go."[39] Shortly thereafter, the accosted Jesus found himself an arm's length from Pontius Pilate and the Roman authorities. As an angry mob outside of Pilate's chambers called for Jesus' life, Pilate inquired of Jesus' kingship. With his life in the balance, Jesus fearlessly responded, "My Kingdom is not an earthly kingdom. If it were, my followers would fight to keep me from being handed over to the Jewish leaders. But my Kingdom is not of this world."[40] Far more than a death certificate, Jesus' words to Pilate were the magnum opus of a good life.

A perfect synthesis of vocation, hope, and social change, his life and death were of equal importance, for they were of "a single respiration."[41] While Jesus' kingship confession before Pilate precipitated the expiration of Jesus' final breath, the inspiration of his short life of alternative resistance can be distilled in a brief formula: "The kingdom of heaven is in us."[42]

According to Thurman, the base of Jesus' formula of resistance "focused on the urgency of radical change in the inner attitude of the people."[43] Lacking protection from ruling authorities, Jesus' revolution began with reclaiming control of the heart.

> Jesus recognized fully that out of the heart are the issues of life and that no external force, however great and overwhelming, can at last long destroy a people if it does not first win the victory of the spirit against them. "To revile because one has been reviled—this is the real evil because it is the evil of the soul itself." Jesus saw this with almighty clarity. Again and again he came back to the inner life of the individual. With increasing insight and startling accuracy he placed his finger on the "inward center" as the crucial arena where the issues would determine the destiny of his people.[44]

From this vantage, Jesus understood that when outside forces control the inner life, the disinherited are backed against the wall and heads remain constantly on swivel. Jesus perceived that with the spirit overtaken, self-worth becomes shackled and questions of fitness, flatness, and belonging confine creative alternatives of change. Further, Jesus grasped that when the inward center rests in the hands of external forces, disequilibrium befuddles the disinherited, and malevolent others gain control of how the uncentered exercise power and respond to crisis.[45] Therefore, under the press of Roman occupation Jesus launched a movement of social change to reclaim the landscape of the inward center.

As a technique of survival for the oppressed, through word and action, Jesus contested social inferiority by impressing a profound sense of belonging upon all (lepers, adulterers, tax collectors, and even Roman soldiers) that crossed within his three-feet orbit. "The core of the analysis of Jesus is that [humans are children] of God, the God of life that sustains all nature and guarantees all the intricacies of the life-process itself."[46] This great affirmation stabilizes personal worth and dignity, and positions the listener "to appraise [one's] own intrinsic powers, gifts, talents, and abilities."[47] The challenge to reappraise one's dignity creates a different lens for the disinherited to assess their present crisis, envision new possibilities, and work toward creating change.

In Thurman's oft-quoted baccalaureate speech "The Sound of the Genuine," he describes an encounter between Jesus and a demon-possessed man. Though the man was sequestered to a living death of rattling his chains in a graveyard on the outskirts of town, Jesus posed two dignity-altering questions that struck the man's inward center: "'Who are you? What is your name?' and for a moment his tilted mind righted itself and he said, 'That's it! I don't know. There are legions of me and they riot in my streets. If I only knew, then I would be whole.'"[48]

By inquiring of the grave-dweller's name, Jesus bestowed upon him dignity and personhood. Scripture further tells us that after driving out the demons, Jesus sent the once-possessed man back home to face those who had marginalized him. Not only was he commissioned to serve as a credible messenger of the healer who welcomed him as a child of God; the once-possessed man was tasked to love those who attempted to destroy him.

Radical in every right, Jesus' said to the disinherited, "Love your enemy." In outlining the taxonomy of hatred, Thurman explains that contact without fellowship leads to unsympathetic understanding, and finally to an active functioning of ill will. To disrupt the breeding of hate, Jesus advocated love.[49] "The first step toward such love is a common sharing of a sense of mutual worth and value."[50] Jesus understood that while the underprivileged remain in constant contact with many who can threaten their well-being, there exists chance opportunities when foes find themselves at arm's length and on common ground.[51] The Samaritan, the tax collector, the Roman soldier, even Pilate himself, stood on different ideological and cultural grounds than Jesus. But through dignifying words and compassionate actions Jesus forged pathways to mutual discovery with unlikely partners. Through this example, Jesus modeled for the oppressed an unwillingness to have his inward center tainted by hate and a refusal to have his soul disfigured by evil opposition.

To be certain, Jesus' position was "deeply resented by many of his fellows, who were suffering as he was."[52] For some, a path of resistance that flowed through the inward center may have seemed acquiescent to the enemy. For others, his alternative may have seemed incapable of making any significant change against the towering house of Rome. However, during his life and for ages following, Jesus' thoughts and actions have served as a compass for the disinherited seeking direction and a template for resistance that exists far beyond the bounds of activism. Knowing that he was and would be both compass and template, he stood before his disciples and teachers of the law and assuredly self-identified: "*I am the way!*"

I Am a Mystic

It felt like heaven, but it was hot as hell. While the ceiling fan had no chance against the three-digit summer heat, my sister teacher's invitation to help catalog her home library placed me at the pearly gates.[53] With universities interested in appraising Ms. Mari's library, she gave me a list and pointed me in the direction to pull the rarest of her collection. Sifting through thousands of books stacked from floor to ceiling, I excavated signed first editions of her sister writers Toni Morrison, Gwendolyn Brooks, Nikki Giovanni, and Maya Angelou. With sweat pouring down my back I continued the dig, and I floated on cloud nine when I uncovered the green-inked personal correspondence from her teacher, Langston Hughes. I sifted through books categorized in history, religion, literature, and law. Then, in the corner of the sweltering attic, I found Howard Thurman's name written on a spine mixed in with a stack of miscellaneous books.

Howard Thurman defied categorization many of his living days. A teacher with an inquisitive mind, in 1935 Thurman voyaged to India and was among the first African Americans to sit in the company of Mohandas Gandhi, discuss tenets of nonviolent direct action, and examine tactics to vitalize the dignity of persons deemed untouchable.[54] Thirteen years later, Thurman published *Jesus and the Disinherited,* which some historians believe Martin Luther King Jr. carried throughout the Montgomery bus boycott[55] and which some activists credit with shaping the philosophy of the civil rights movement.[56] In 1953, *Life* magazine recognized Thurman as one of the twelve greatest preachers of the twentieth century.[57] Given his credentials as an ambassador for his people, an accomplished author, and an acclaimed preacher, many thought at "last someone has come who would be our Moses."[58] But Howard Thurman resisted the categories that might label him as a front-page activist for causes of racial justice. He sought another way to resist the social ills.

Like Jesus, who was conditioned by birth to live among the disinherited, Howard Thurman as an African American in the segregated South also moved on the margins of society. As a sensitive child, Thurman suffered much from the racial violence in his hometown of Daytona. When "life became more and more suffocating because of fear of being brutalized, beaten or otherwise outraged," Thurman turned within and sought control of resources that were accessible to him and God alone.[59] By claiming his inner landscape, young man Howard laid the ground that soon led him to declare, "*I am a mystic.*"

In order to understand the lifework of a mystic, one must first define mysticism. For ages, theologians have sought to distinguish mystical experience from metaphysical doctrines of the soul. For the purposes of this book, I am less concerned about the latter. In this regard, I side with the renowned Quaker mystic and scholar Rufus Jones, who states, "I am not interested in mysticism as an 'ism.' It turns out in most accounts to be a dry and abstract thing. . . . It is mystical experience and not mysticism that is worthy of our study."[60] To this end, I have derived the following understanding of how the mystic's experiences heighten consciousness and inform relationships with God and the world. The mystic perceives that the ultimate dwells within finite experience; therefore, careful examination of one's life can disclose truths, yield wisdom, and unlock revelations about humanity, nature, and God.[61] Three fundamental convictions frame this assertion:

1. In the essence of all life and creation there is an underlying spirituality.
2. The soul as well as the eye can perceive and have direct and unmediated interaction with God. Therefore, revelatory insights from the living God are attainable even without the conduit of institutional religion.[62] Additionally, through this perceptive spiritual sense the soul can pass from the temporal to the Eternal.[63]
3. Unlike the dissociative qualities of mental illness, mysticism is inherently integrative such that connection with the living God can deepen discernment and enhance relationship with others and self.[64]

While a heightened mystical consciousness enables unique pathways to discern God's presence and will, accompanying the mystic's
spiritual gift of perception also comes a social responsibility to care and
serve. As "spiritual issues are the very ground of all material issues (e.g.
politics, civil rights, poverty, crime),"[65] the mystic bears the weight
and commitment of utilizing spiritual attunement to call out injustice,
negotiate peace, and create pockets of resistance. In response to these
commitments, the mystic engages in the work of building the kingdom
of God on earth as it is in heaven.[66]

Guided by the wisdom of Jesus, the tutelage of teachers, and a host
of transcendent personal encounters, Thurman as a mystic located
within himself "the door that no man could shut" and discovered that
even under siege he could retain "the equilibrium and the tranquility
of inner peace."[67] As a path of resistance, Thurman employed mystical insights to help others "restore and discover self-worth"[68] and "to
remove anything that prevented the individual free and easy access to
the [inward center]."[69] Thurman's mystical approach to social change
moves within the individual, between communities, and beneath the
surface of the evil order.

In *Deep Is the Hunger* Thurman asked the ever-pressing question of
souls assaulted by oppressive systems: "*What is it that we want and need
in order to be worthful persons in our own sight?*"[70] Taking cues from
Jesus and Gandhi, who both sought to dispel notions of inferiority
lodged within the hearts of children of God, Thurman believed that
transforming how individuals perceived themselves was the first step
in remaking the social order.[71] Since the battle for self-worth is waged
within, Thurman stressed the power of daily decision making. In a
brief reflection, just a few pages after his question on finding worth,
Thurman contended that all humans are confronted with options that
reveal "a philosophy of living." Even in times of social upheaval, decisions can be made on when the body rests and when it wakes. For the
rich and poor alike, choices on how money is allocated reveal values.
Furthermore, decisions on relational presence, allocation of energy,
and pursuit of vocation demonstrate volitional power.[72] So Thurman
devoted many of his writings, speeches, and sermons to helping individuals move within and take ownership of seemingly insignificant
daily decisions as assertive acts of defining self-worth.

On the campus of Eden Seminary in October 1978, Thurman
delivered a lecture titled "Mysticism and Social Action." Among the
key themes in his lecture was the obligation of the spiritually sensitive

person not to lose a sense of "particularity." His concept of particularity suggests that regardless of one's lot in life, every person should be seen as a subject and not an object, as a particular human being and not representative of a larger body. For example, it is possible to feed the hungry and lose sight of the particular famished person. In this regard, by not seeing the particular hungry individual, the act of caring torments the one in need. The same is true for the outsized who look in the face of giants and fail to realize that systems are made of particular persons who must be seen and held accountable for their individual actions against others.

Recognizing that human contact without fellowship between particular persons breeds a cycle of hatred, Thurman saw the need to create communal spaces for mutual discovery, where unlikely partners might search for common ground. In the broader scope of history, such person-to-person resistance may seem inconsequential. Yet consider this: In 1944, as Jim Crow laws governed social spaces and individual interactions, Thurman and a white Presbyterian clergyman named Rev. Alfred Fisk founded the nation's first interfaith, interracial congregation. Over time, Thurman's sermons would be broadcast nationwide. Ever so slowly he chipped away at an oppressive system built on diminishing particularity and driving a wedge between unlikely partners. A seemingly small ripple can indeed become a wave.

Thurman's approach to activism not only sought to vitalize individual self-worth and create spaces of mutual discovery between unlikely partners; it also sought to move beneath the evil order. In a recorded meditation titled "Those Who Walked with God" Thurman laid out how mystics can channel the power of God through word and deed to subvert systems of oppression:

> [Mystics] do not withdraw from the struggle, but they feel the way to do it is to move underneath the foundation that stabilizes the evil order. And if you move at that level, when you stir, everything that is above you will begin to crumble and fall because there is no power less than the power of God that is capable of withstanding the power of God. Therefore, if I can release as a living channel, a living energy, of God into the situation, anything that is in the situation will be destroyed.
>
> That is what the mystic does as social action. He is no coward, sticking his head in the sand. Praying to God because he is scared or because he does not have the nerve to do anything else. But he is sure that he is in touch with terrible energy. And if his life can be a

point of focus through which that energy hits its mark in the world, then the redemptive process can work. That is why the way of the mystic is so difficult and yet in some ways so simple.[73]

The work of Fearless Dialogues continues in the lineage of Thurman's mystical tradition by calling individuals to be mindful of small decisions, by challenging communities not to shun particularity, and by using the Laboratory of Discovery to artistically release a living channel, a living energy of God, to destabilize the foundations of evil resting in the hearts and minds of others.

I Am an Artist

We were crossing the Mojave Desert in a two-seater when the aftershock of my vocational crisis hit. Miles away from the bustling cities, I looked out from the passenger seat onto the dry parched land. Before me a seemingly endless road. To the left and right, sand, rocks, and high cliffs as far as the eye could see. Then, with a certain suddenness, I lost my breath. Gasping for air and suffocating by paradox, I felt closed in by the vast, open space of the wilderness. Never stricken by asthma or immobilizing anxiety, I turned to my youngest brother behind the wheel. "I think I'm having a panic attack!" Channeling a sagacious calmness like the desert fathers of old, Jahmel called my name and instructed, "Gregory, just breathe."

Hours after the tremors of my vocational crisis calmed, I asked Jahmel to pull the two-seater over onto the highway shoulder. As we came to a rolling stop, the gravel crunched under the tires, and a dust cloud bellowed around the car. I cracked the door, and the dry desert heat rushed into the vehicle, proving its dominance over the cool streams pushing through the air-conditioned vents. Just steps away from the car, with rocky sand underfoot, the setting sun appeared as painted watercolors across the desert sky. Lavender, fuchsia, hues of green and orange blended across the horizon. Then it happened. While beholding the setting sun, it dawned upon me . . . *I am an artist!*

Though I was standing on dry, parched land, creative possibilities of being in the world beyond the confines of scholar, minister, and activist flooded to the fore. I don't paint, draw, or sing. But like a master potter at the sculptor's wheel I create spaces for hard conversations. Like an iron chef at play, I stand in pulpits and mix Scripture with music, drama, abstract theories, and folk wisdom to help the faithful see invisible people hidden in plain view. Like a museum curator assembling rare collections, one-third of every class I teach is off campus, so that students can hear the untold stories of master practitioners who bind communities together with little recognition. Like an imaginative child with crayons in hand, I sketch visions of an interrupting hope in the minds of business tycoons, gang leaders, and activists, who have been pummeled by the Big Three. I am an artist who teaches, preaches, and acts upon conviction to create spaces that catalyze change.

Can you grant yourself the freedom to dream beyond the tight boxes of vocation? How might your service to the world look different, sound different, feel different, if you unhinged your creativity and your efforts to fit the norm? What would our world, our communities, our families be like if small cadres of the "vocationally uncategorizable" committed to band together and change the three feet around them?

I Am an Interrupter

I devote the entire fourth chapter of my first book, *Cut Dead but Still Alive*, to exploring how an interrupting hope foils the woeful ills of despair, apathy, and shame. As defined in the text, "an interrupting hope is a disruptive desire for existential change that is generated and sustained in a community of reliable others that names difficulties, envisions new possibilities, and inspires work toward transformation of self and other."[74] This definition proves so central to the work of seeing the invisible and hearing the muted that I definitively state, "Interruption lies at the heart of hope and is the bloodline pulsing through [the] entire book."[75]

> An interrupting hope actively disrupts the mundane, predictable, and routine by interjecting a new outlook and way of being. This concept of disruptively halting the continuous progress of hopelessness emerged from examining the work of Gary Slutkin and his colleagues at CeaseFire.
>
> Slutkin, a medical doctor who spent most of his career fighting epidemic diseases such as tuberculosis, cholera, and AIDS with the World Health Organization, proposed that the epidemic of violence could be contained like a contagious disease [if transmission could be interrupted]. . . . Slutkin explains that in a flu epidemic doctors immunize to block transmission. To block the transmission of

violence, Slutkin's organization developed a "cadre of workers called the violence interrupters who can detect and interrupt events and block one of them from leading to another."[76]

Violence interrupters move toward the place where violence is nearing eruption; then they literally place their bodies between the warring factions to immunize violence and broker peace. The violence interrupters, comprised of former gang members with street credibility, serve as a disruptive stopgap in the heat of rage. Each CeaseFire interruption faces a difficulty, envisions a possibility beyond violence, and takes a risk to create change. My boyhood hero lived a good life and died a good death adhering to such a philosophy.

In those early days of kindergarten, Brandon interrupted the cycle of bullying and infused hope in my life when he stood between me and the Big Three—despair, apathy, and shame. A dozen years later, Brandon put his body between two warring factions to interrupt another violent cycle. Others at that postgame hot spot could have intervened. They did not. Yet young man Brandon declaratively knew, "*I am an interrupter.*"

Had Brandon not stood between me and my kindergarten bullies, or between those hotheaded teens intent on harming each other, much of my life would have been different. While I never heard Brandon call himself an activist, his interruptions changed the three feet around him, wherever he went. I contend that hope-igniting interruptions are kindled by a divine spark within that compels our eyes to see the invisible, and trains our ears to hear the muted who stand with their backs against the wall. With clarified vision, attuned hearing, and hearts aflame, activism expands beyond a set of actions and becomes a way of being, a way of living, a way of moving in the world as an interrupter.

Can you feel the warm flame of interruption growing in your belly?

I Am Fearless Dialogues

Fearless Dialogues is far more than a series of theory-based experiments. It is a lifelong inward journey that manifests itself in how individuals change the world around them in three-feet increments. Fearless Dialogues' artistic way of resistance challenges unlikely partners to face the Big Three that bully from within, so that they may move fearlessly to spark interruptions in their daily lives. It is our belief that in time these incremental changes shake the foundations of oppressive systems that tower over the outsized, who live with their heads on swivel.

Like striking the abrasive edge of a matchbox, Fearless Dialogues animators seek to scratch the subconscious of unlikely partners, so they may consider how to interrupt the Big Three on a daily basis in their homes, schools, workplaces, and communities. For some unlikely partners, ignition occurs from experiencing Radical Hospitality, engaging art in the Living Museum, or exploring theories of invisibility, marginalization, and ostracism. For others, flicker turns to flame when facing the Five Hardest Questions or while taking a Long Loving Look at the Real. In the Laboratory of Discovery these experiments smolder in the hearts of unlikely partners; but once they return to their communities, the flame gains oxygen, and a wildfire within clears a path of new questions for life to start afresh.

How might we employ Radical Hospitality in our daily interactions with Public Strangers whom we encounter on our morning commute, with Familiar Strangers whom we sit next to in crowded classrooms, and with Intimate Strangers who grace our lives when we least expect?

How might our parental engagement with our school-age children deepen if we looked at television, movies, and magazine images as part of a Living Museum, and asked our school-age teachers: Who do you see? Who don't you hear? Where is hope?

How might our organizational understandings be altered if senior and support staff wrestled with theories of marginality and ostracism by inquiring together: What does it feel like to be cut dead, to be muted, to be invisible? How can we create an organizational ethos that supports our fundamental human needs of belonging, control, self-esteem, and meaningful existence?

How might we create spaces in our homes, churches, and temples, to face life's hardest questions? How might our sense of identity, purpose, and legacy change if these seemingly insular communities asked: Who are we? What is our gift? What must we do to die a good death?

How might we alter the harried pace of our daily schedules to take a Long Loving Look at unlikely partners from different faiths, political ideologies, sexual orientations, or socioeconomic backgrounds?

Finally, in an age when civil conversations in the media often devolve into punitive punditry and divisive debate, how might we engage in Fearless Dialogues that spark flames of hope and change the three feet around us?

If these questions swell your flame, whisper to yourself, "*I am Fearless Dialogues!*"

A FINAL WORD: ON CHANGE, THREE FEET AT A TIME

For far too long, the behemoths of racism and classism and the mammoths of sexism and ageism have cast shadows on the outsized and distorted vocations of resistance. But you, Beloved Reader, are in close proximity to these words. It is my prayer that from your reading a spark is smoldering that will serve as a pillar of fire to traverse the shadow. I am not calling for you, Beloved Reader, to change the world. Yet I beckon you to hear the wisdom of my Aunt Dotty, who more than three decades ago unknowingly set the course for Fearless Dialogues, with these words: "I don't know how to change the world. But I can change the three feet around me." So, as we go forth from these pages, to extend Radical Hospitality, face hard questions, interrupt the Big Three, and live fearlessly, let us do so, three feet at a time.

Notes

Chapter 1: Fear+Less Dialogues Introduced

1. Kevin Quashie, *Sovereignty of Quiet: Beyond Resistance in Black Culture* (Piscataway, NJ: Rutgers University Press, 2012), 4.

2. Parker J. Palmer, *To Know as We Are Known: Education as a Spiritual Journey* (San Francisco: Harper & Row, 1983), 5.

3. Seni Tienabeso, Matt Gutman, and Stephanie Wash, "George Zimmerman Found Not Guilty and Goes Free," *ABC News,* July 13, 2013, *http*://abcnews.go .com/US/george-zimmerman-found-guilty-free/story?id=19653300.

4. *Daily News* Staff, "George Zimmerman Verdict: Twitter Erupts After Ex-Neighborhood Watchman Walks on Trayvon Martin Murder Charge," *New York Daily News,* July 13, 2013, http://www.nydailynews.com/news/national /george-zimmerman-verdict-twitter-erupts-ex-neighborhood-watchman-walks -murder-charge-article-1.1398213.

5. Ryan Devereaux, "No Justice: Thousands March for Trayvon Martin," *Rolling Stone,* July 15, 2013, http://www.rollingstone.com/politics/news/no-justice -thousands-march-for-trayvon-martin-20130715.

6. Jehmu Greene, "After Zimmerman Verdict, Trayvon Martin Isn't Only Victim," *Fox News Opinion,* July 17, 2013, http://www.foxnews.com/opinion /2013/07/17/after-zimmerman-verdict-trayvon-martin-isnt-only-victim.html.

7. Tom Cohen, "Obama: Trayvon Martin Could Have Been Me," *CNN Politics,* July 19, 2013, http://www.cnn.com/2013/07/19/politics/obama-zimmerman/.

8. Jeffrey Weiss, "White Churches Uncommonly Quiet after Zimmerman Verdict," *CNN Belief Blog,* July 20, 2013, http://religion.blogs.cnn .com/2013/07/20/on-zimmerman-verdict-a-loud-silence-from-white-churches/.

9. In the words of Parker Palmer, the name tags serve the purpose of leveling the playing field of conversation, so that participants in dialogue meet "soul-to-soul" and not "role-to-role." A host of techniques, structured around Radical Hospitality, is employed to ensure that both dominant and marginal persons are fully seen and heard.

10. Howard Thurman, *Jesus and the Disinherited* (Boston: Beacon Press, 1996), 36.

11. Thurman, *Jesus and the Disinherited,* 37.

12. Studies show that when persons feel unacknowledged, the fundamental human needs of belonging, self-esteem, control, and a sense of meaningful

existence are threatened. If these fundamental needs are in question, it is most unlikely that head-to-heart conversations like the ones in the four vignettes above will occur. For a summary of Kipling Williams' four fundamental human needs and the adverse effect of their absence on persons who are unseen and unheard, see Gregory C. Ellison II, *Cut Dead but Still Alive: Caring for African American Men* (Nashville: Abingdon Press, 2013), 22–24.

13. Barbara Brown Taylor, *Learning to Walk in the Dark* (New York: Harper One, 2014), 92.

Chapter 2: Conversations with Country Dark

1. James Weldon Johnson, *God's Trombones: Seven Negro Sermons in Verse*, ed. Henry Louis Gates Jr. (New York: Penguin, 2008), 17.

2. In his psychoanalytic interpretation of caves, Harold P. Blum likens the underground cavernous spaces inhabited by our Paleolithic ancestors to the birth canal or womb where living organisms produced undying art. Furthermore, exiting the cave was a dangerous proposition, as the living being left the security of the comforting object (Harold P. Blum, "The Psychological Birth of Art: A Psychoanalytic Approach to Prehistoric Cave Art," *International Forum of Psychoanalysis* 20, no. 4 [2011], 201).

3. While the earliest known rock art, found in Africa, dates from nearly 75,000 years ago, art historians date prehistoric cave art in select locations in France and Spain as less than 40,000 years old (Blum, "Psychological Birth of Art," 196).

4. John Halverson suggests that cave artists largely portrayed animals that posed little threat to our prehistoric forebears. He explains, "The subject matter of this art, so far as it is representational, is overwhelmingly animals. A good number of humans . . . and perhaps a few plants are depicted, but the vast majority are animals, and of these, the great majority are large, edible herbivores, especially horse and bison, and also cattle, deer, ibex, mammoth and rhinoceros; more rarely depicted are felines, bears, fish, birds, and reptiles" (John Halverson, "Paleolithic Art and Cognition," *The Journal of Psychology* 126, no. 3 [1992]: 222).

Blum offers a grimmer picture and explains that in addition to renderings of docile herbivores, the images on cave walls also portrayed animals that posed a more immediate threat. He believes that the animals painted with such lifelike virtuosity were those observed, hunted, feared, and perhaps honored or worshiped by prehistoric humans. They include the extinct mammoth, wooly rhinoceros, auroch (a fierce oversized ox), giant elk, horse, bison, reindeer, bear, unidentified herbivores, and rarely fish, for example a salmon." His inclusion of fear-inducing predators suggests that cave artists were utilizing art to process external stimuli that potentially threatened their existence. Blum further posits that carve art may have also been "counterphobic" against frightening nightmares, haunting imagery, and ancestral ghosts of the supernatural world (Blum, "Psychological Birth of Art," 202).

5. Blum, "Psychological Birth of Art," 200.

6. Ibid., 196–97.

7. Ibid., 200. While Blum's research focuses primarily on the discoveries of cave art in France and Spain, Sven Ouzman, a rock art researcher from the University of Western Australia, details how 14,000 years ago members of the San society in the heartland of central South Africa hammered, rubbed, cut, and flaked rock in order to produce sound. Like the cave art discussed in this chapter, the rock-art sites provided the San societies opportunity to contemplate, question, and make sense of both the ordinary world, where people physically dwelt, and the spirit world, where God, the spirits of the dead, supernatural people, and potent animals existed (Sven Ouzman, "Seeing Is Deceiving: Rock Art and the Non-Visual," *World Archaeology* 33, no. 2 [2001]: 237–38).

8. Barbara Brown Taylor, "The Bright Cloud of Unknowing," Day1.org, March 2, 2014, http://day1.org/5560-the_bright_cloud_of_unknowing.

9. Ibid.

10. Ibid.

11. Ibid.

12. Ibid.

13. Dr. Seuss, *Green Eggs and Ham* (New York: Beginner Books, Random House, 1988), 16.

14. Barbara Brown Taylor, *The Preaching Life* (Cambridge: Cowley Publications, 1993), 41.

15. Ibid.

16. Ibid., 42.

17. Ibid.

18. Ibid., 41.

19. Barbara Brown Taylor, *An Altar in the World* (New York: Harper One, 2009), 30.

20. Ibid., 56.

21. Ibid., 120.

22. Ibid., 32.

23. Ibid., 40.

24. Ibid., 19.

25. Ibid.

26. Ibid., 20.

27. Ibid., 22–23, 27.

28. Ibid., 21.

29. Anne C. Loveland and Otis B. Wheeler, *From Meetinghouse to Megachurch: A Material and Cultural History* (Columbia: University of Missouri Press, 2003), 91.

30. In certain African traditions, the Chakaba don sacred garb and dance on stilts to bless spaces and dispel negativity. Some traditions also surmise that the height of the stilt walker reminds us to look up to the ancestors who came before. For more information on Chakaba see Kariamu Welsh-Asante, ed. *African Dance: An Artistic, Historical, and Philosophical Inquiry* (Trenton, NJ: Africa World Press, 1998), 25.

Chapter 3: The Welcome Table of Radical Hospitality

1. Arnold Rampersad, ed., "I've Known Rivers," in *The Collected Poems of Langston Hughes,* (New York: Vintage Books, 1994), 23.

2. Throughout the book, I capitalize the words Public Stranger, Familiar Stranger, Intimate Stranger, and the Stranger Within, because the terms are utilized as proper nouns that represent individuals and groups who participate in Fearless Dialogues conversations. In this footnote and throughout this chapter, I credit Parker J. Palmer, Stanley Milgram, and Robert C. Dykstra as the theorists who developed the terms Public Stranger, Familiar Stranger, and Intimate Stranger, respectively.

3. Henri Nouwen, *Reaching Out: The Three Movements of the Spiritual Life* (Garden City, NY: Doubleday, 1975), 46.

4. Ibid., 47.

5. Parker J. Palmer, *The Company of Strangers: Christians and the Renewal of America's Public Life* (New York: Crossroad, 1981), 58.

6. For more information on the stories of hardship and sacrifice during the Great Migration of African Americans from the southernmost regions of the United States northward, see Isabel Wilkerson, *The Warmth of Other Suns: The Epic Story of America's Great Migration* (New York: Vintage Books, 2011).

7. Palmer, *The Company of Strangers*, 35.

8. Ibid., 38–39.

9. Ibid., 42.

10. D. W. Winnicott, *Playing and Reality* (New York: Routledge, 2005), 10.

11. Stephen A. Mitchell and Margaret J. Black, *Freud and Beyond: A History of Modern Psychoanalytic Thought* (New York: Basic Books, 2016), 126, italics added.

12. Ibid.

13. Ibid., 127.

14. Winnicott, *Playing and Reality*, 3.

15. Ibid., 4.

16. Ibid.

17. Stanley Milgram, *The Individual in a Social World: Essays and Experiments* (London: Pinter & Martin, 2010), 29–33.

18. Ibid., 42–55.

19. Ibid., 60.

20. Ibid.

21. Ibid., 60–62.

22. Ibid., 62.

23. "Greyhound" is a colloquial abbreviation for Greyhound Lines, an inter-city bus carrier with more than 2,700 destinations in the United States.

24. Milgram, *The Individual in a Social World*, 62.

25. Robert C. Dykstra, "Intimate Strangers: The Role of Hospital Chaplains in Situations of Sudden Traumatic Loss," *Journal of Pastoral Care* 44, no. 2 (1990): 139.

26. Ibid., 148.

27. Ibid., 131.

28. In an amazing, hilarious display of cultural analysis, comedian Chris Rock uncovers the lack of appreciation and attention afforded to many African American fathers of his generation. In this particular skit in his HBO stand-up special titled *Bigger and Blacker* (1999), Rock discloses that all the "ready daddy gets for all his work is the big piece of chicken."

29. D. W. Winnicott, "Cure," quoted in Adam Phillips, *Winnicott* (Cambridge: Harvard University Press, 1988), 11.

30. Dykstra, "Intimate Stranger," 124.

31. Ibid.

32. Ibid., 135.

33. Walter Earl Fluker and Catherine Tumber, eds., "How Good It Is to Center Down," in *A Strange Freedom: The Best of Howard Thurman and Religious Experience* (Boston: Beacon Press, 1998), 305.

34. Nouwen, *Reaching Out*, 53.

35. Rogers's title is inspired by a quote that he came across in Søren Kierkegaard, *The Sickness unto Death* (Princeton: Princeton University Press, 1941), 29.

36. Carl Rogers, *On Becoming a Person: A Therapist's View of Psychotherapy* (Boston: Houghton Mifflin, 1961), 167.

37. Ibid., 168.

38. Gregory C. Ellison II, *Cut Dead but Still Alive: Caring for African American Young Men* (Nashville: Abingdon Press, 2013), 56.

39. While not given treatment in this chapter, Rogers finds that his clients also made the moves away from meeting expectations and pleasing others. See Rogers, *On Becoming a Person*, 169–70.

40. Ibid., 173.

41. Ibid. Also not addressed in this chapter are Rogers's movements toward self-direction, being process, being complexity, and trust of self.

42. Ibid. Rogers's carefully worded explanation of the epiphanies experienced by clients undergirds my understanding and articulation of how the Stranger Within becomes integrated in the whole of the self . . . and, for this I am grateful.

43. Ibid., 174.

44. Nouwen, *Reaching Out*, 53.

45. Not until many years later did I come to realize that this "church song" was indeed a folk song composed at the Highlander Folk School. The leaders at Highlander taught this song to the students of SNCC, and the eschatological imagination of these words would embolden the collegians to remain steadfast as they staged sit-ins at lunch counters and were categorically unwelcomed by the management and dining clientele.

Chapter 4: When Pupils See

1. Paul Laurence Dunbar, "We Wear the Mask," in *The Complete Poems of Paul Laurence Dunbar* (New York: Dodd, Mead, and Co., 1922), 71.

2. Jane Vella, *Learning to Listen, Listening to Teach: The Power of Dialogue in Educating Adults* (San Francisco: Jossey-Bass, 2002), 10.

3. Ibid.

4. Kipling D. Williams, *Ostracism: The Power of Silence* (New York: Guilford Press, 2001), 1–2.

5. The following semester, I took a course on psychobiography taught by Dr. Capps. Uncharacteristically, he allowed me to revise the course syllabus and replace three required texts with books that I deemed more relevant to the African American context. That summer, Dr. Capps asked to reread every paper that I had submitted to him that year. By summer's end, he mailed the papers to my home with a second level of comments. Long before my days as a doctoral student and a professor, Dr. Capps *saw* something in me. His thoughtful feedback and investment in my becoming a better writer proved pivotal in my development. For this I am grateful. Dr. Capps, may you rest in peace.

6. Capps frames James as a religious melancholic, who worries about the remote future of the world but possesses a philosophically deeper understanding of God than religious idealists. Referring to James's pivotal chapter, "Sick Soul," in *Varieties of Religious Experience,* Capps explores the psychological and religious overtones of melancholia. He extracts two examples from this chapter to make this point. The first is that of a French mental patient, symbolizing the materialists, who was afraid of God and was led to a life of despair, panic fear, and near suicide. The second example refers to James himself, a religious melancholiac/idealist, who in grappling with panic found hope in biblical assurances that God was his refuge. In the latter example, the texts of Scripture functioned psychologically for James and made a decisive difference in his mental stability and survival. See Donald Capps, "The Letting Loose of Hope: Where Psychology of Religion and Pastoral Care Converge," *Journal of Pastoral Care* 51 (1997): 139–49.

7. William James, *The Principles of Psychology* (New York: H. Holt & Co., 1890), 292–93, emphasis added.

8. African American young men are particularly susceptible.

9. Gregory C. Ellison II, *Cut Dead but Still Alive: Caring for African American Young Men* (Nashville: Abingdon Press, 2013).

10. Howard Thurman, *Inward Journey* (New York: Harper, 1961).

11. Ibid., 61.

12. Ibid.

13. Kipling D. Williams, Joseph P. Forgas, and William Von Hippel, eds., *The Social Outcast: Ostracism, Social Exclusion, Rejection, and Bullying* (New York: Psychology Press, 2005), 22. For more information on the necessity of belonging for human flourishing, see Baumeister and Leary, "The Need to Belong: Desire for Interpersonal Attachments as a Fundamental Human Motivation," *Psychological Bulletin* 177, no. 3 (1995): 497–529.

14. Williams, *Ostracism,* 62.

15. Ibid., 65.

16. Ibid., 63.

17. Proverbs 20:12.

18. Williams, *Ostracism*, 1–2.

19. Parker J. Palmer, *A Hidden Wholeness: The Journey toward an Undivided Life: Welcoming the Soul and Weaving Community in a Wounded World* (San Francisco: Jossey-Bass, 2004), 58.

Chapter 5: Listening for the Love Below

1. Lucille Clifton, "Seeker of Visions," in *The Collected Poems of Lucille Clifton 1965–2010*, ed. Kevin Young and Michael S. Glaser (Rochester: BOA Editions, 2012), 453.

2. James A. Vela-McConnell, *Who Is My Neighbor?: Social Affinity in the Modern World* (Albany: State University of New York Press, 1999), 8.

3. Ibid., 7; emphasis added.

4. Ibid., 8.

5. Ibid., 9.

6. Ibid., 10.

7. Ibid.

8. Walter J. Burghardt, "Contemplation: A Long Loving Look at the Real," *Church* 5, (winter 1989): 14.

9. I was introduced to the Long Loving Look at the Real experiment by my dear friend and colleague Rahiel Tesfamariam. I initially utilized this experiment in workshops and in my classrooms at Candler School of Theology. Over time, the Fearless Dialogues team has adapted and revised the experiment's instructions

and debriefing to meet the needs of unlikely partners and strengthen connections between seemingly disparate groups at community conversations.

10. Burghardt, "Contemplation: A Long Loving Look at the Real," 15.

11. James Melvin Washington, ed., "A Christmas Sermon on Peace," in *A Testament of Hope: The Essential Writings and Speeches of Martin Luther King, Jr.* (San Francisco: HarperSanFrancisco, 1991), 254.

12. Burghardt, "Contemplation: A Long Loving Look at the Real," 16.

13. Ibid.

14. Mari Evans, "Celebration," *A Dark and Splendid Mass* (New York: Harlem River Press, 1993), 20–21.

15. Recognizing that silent eyes tell a story, individuals often respond that they have heard untold stories of strength, perseverance, and determination, lying behind the pupils of people they do not know.

16. Burghardt, "Contemplation: A Long Loving Look at the Real," 14–16.

17. William James, *The Principles of Psychology* (New York: H. Holt & Co., 1890), 292–93.

18. Henri Nouwen, *The Selfless Way of Christ: Downward Mobility and the Spiritual Life* (Maryknoll, NY: Orbis, 2012), 49.

19. Ibid.

20. Karen Scheib, *Pastoral Theology: Telling the Stories of Our Lives* (Nashville: Abingdon Press, 2016), 64.

21. Ibid., 62.

22. Ibid., 63.

23. Ibid., 63–64.

24. Ibid., 64.

25. Ibid., 63.

26. Ibid., 64–65.

27. Ibid., 65.

28. Ibid.

29. Parker J. Palmer, *A Hidden Wholeness: The Journey toward an Undivided Life: Welcoming the Soul and Weaving Community in a Wounded World* (San Francisco: Jossey-Bass, 2004), 27.

30. Ibid., 25.

31. Ibid., 23.

32. Ibid., 65.

33. Ibid.

34. Ibid., 26.

35. Ibid., 120.

36. Deborah Cramer, *The Great Waters: An Atlantic Passage* (New York: W. W. Norton, 2001), 184.

37. Rebecca Hersher, "The Universe Has Almost 10 Times More Galaxies Than We Thought," National Public Radio, npr.com, October 14, 2016.

38. Thomas Duffy, "Crystallography's Journey to the Deep Earth," *Nature* 506, no. 7489 (2014): 429.

39. Edgar H. Schein, *Humble Inquiry: The Gentle Art of Asking instead of Telling* (San Francisco: Berrett Koehler, 2013), 2.

40. Ibid., 4.

41. Ibid., 9.

42. Parker J. Palmer, *The Courage to Teach: Guide for Reflection and Renewal* (San Francisco: Jossey-Bass, 1999), 126.

43. Schein, *Humble Inquiry*, 41.

44. Palmer, *The Courage to Teach*, 126.

45. Ibid.

46. Parker J. Palmer, *The Courage to Teach: Exploring the Inner Landscape of a Teacher's Life* (San Francisco: Jossey-Bass, 2017), 156.

47. Rainer Maria Rilke, *Letters to a Young Poet* (Novato, CA: New World Library, 2000), 35.

48. Palmer, *A Hidden Wholeness*, 120.

49. Psalm 139:8, New International Reader's Version.

Chapter 6: To Die a Good Death

1. "The Third Sermon on the Warpland," in *The Essential Gwendolyn Brooks,* ed. Elizabeth Alexander (New York: Library of America, 2005), 101–2.

2. Howard Thurman, *Jesus and the Disinherited* (Boston: Beacon Press, 1996), 35.

3. Howard Thurman, *The Inward Journey: The Writings of Howard Thurman* (Richmond, IN: Friends United Press, 1971), 71.

4. I am grateful to fellow writer friends Bernard Kynes, Iyabo Onipede, Patrick Reyes, Toby Sanders, and Matthew Williams, who encouraged me with probing questions about this chapter to dislodge me from my writer's block.

5. Erik H. Erikson, *Young Man Luther: A Study in Psychoanalysis and History* (New York: W. W. Norton, 1958), 23.

6. Ibid., 38.

7. Personal Conversation with Luther Smith on December 14, 2016, emphasis added.

8. Luther E. Smith, *Howard Thurman: The Mystic as Prophet* (Richmond, IN: Friends United Press, 1991), 39.

9. Ibid.

10. Howard Thurman, "My People Need Me," in *The Papers of Howard Washington Thurman*, ed. W. E. Fluker (Columbia: University of South Carolina Press, 2009), 1–3.

11. Howard Thurman, *With Head and Heart: The Autobiography of Howard Thurman* (New York: Harcourt Brace Jovanovich, 1979), 24–25.

12. Thurman, "My People Need Me," 1.

13. Ibid., 2.

14. Ibid.

15. Thurman, *With Head and Heart*, 49–50.

16. Known at the time as Ceylon.

17. Thurman, *Jesus and the Disinherited*, 15.

18. Luther E. Smith, "Howard Thurman," in *Christian Spirituality: The Classics*, ed. Arthur Holder (New York: Routledge, 2009), 342.

19. I supplement these three points made in *Jesus and the Disinherited* with references to this subject in an earlier convocation address given by Thurman in the summer of 1935 titled "Good News for the Underprivileged." I find it intriguing that Thurman had done the preliminary research and delivered this talk on the religion of Jesus months prior to his conversation with the Hindu administrator. One could only imagine that Thurman made mention of the remarks from this convocation lecture during the five-hour fearless dialogue. See Howard Thurman, "Good News for the Underprivileged," in *The Papers of Howard Washington Thurman*, ed. W. E. Fluker (Columbia: University of South Carolina Press, 2009), 263–69.

20. Thurman, *Jesus and the Disinherited*, 16.

21. Ibid., 15–16.

22. Ibid., 17.

23. Ibid., 33.

24. Ibid., 22–23.

25. Ibid., 23.

26. Ibid.

27. Ibid.

28. Ibid., 26.

29. Howard Thurman, *Temptations of Jesus: Five Sermons Given in Marsh Chapel, Boston University, 1962* (Richmond, IN: Friends United Press, 1997), 18.

30. "Apathy is the state of not caring about what is happening around us, to us, or within us. This threat stands counter to the hoping process that is fueled by desire, because the apathetic person is unaware of having any desires." For more on apathy, see Gregory C. Ellison II, *Cut Dead but Still Alive: Caring for African American Young Men* (Nashville: Abingdon Press, 2013), 92–93.

31. Thurman, *Temptations of Jesus*, 27.

32. Matt. 9:10.

33. Matt. 8:3.

34. John 4:9.

35. Matt. 8:5–13.

36. Matt. 12:9–12.

37. John 8:1–7 (NLT).

38. Matt. 21:12–13.

39. John 18:2–8.

40. John 18:28–36 (NLT).

41. Thurman, *Inward Journey*, 71.

42. Thurman, *Jesus and the Disinherited*, 27.

43. Ibid., 21.

44. Ibid.

45. Ibid., 28.

46. Ibid., 49.

47. Ibid., 53.

48. Howard Thurman, "The Sound of the Genuine," in *Crossings Reflection* 4 (Indianapolis: University of Indianapolis, 1902), http://eip.uindy.edu/crossings /publications/reflection4.pdf.

49. Thurman, *Jesus and the Disinherited*, 75–78.

50. Ibid., 98.

51. Ibid., 101.

52. Ibid., 28.

53. My beloved sister teacher, and Yoda, Mari Evans breathed her last breath on March 10, 2017. Hours before her transition, I submitted the draft of this manuscript to my editor. I am grateful for her wisdom, wit, and love. Deep in my heart, I believe that she was with me then and now, as this work makes its way into the world. I love you, Ms. Mari.

54. Thurman, *With Head and Heart*, 101. For more information on Thurman's travels to India, see Quinton Dixie and Peter Eisenstadt, *Visions of a Better World* (Boston: Beacon Press, 2011).

55. Smith, *The Mystic as Prophet*, 140–41. In connecting Thurman's writings with the work of Martin Luther King Jr., Smith references an interview between King and historian Lerone Bennett Jr.

56. In reference to Thurman's influence on the philosophy of nonviolent direct action, Smith captures the sentiments of noted civil rights activist Otis Moss, who states: "It might be that he [Thurman] did not join the march from Selma to Montgomery, or many of the other marches, but he has participated at the level that shapes the philosophy that creates the march—and without that people don't know what to do before they march, while they march, or after they march" (Smith, *The Mystic as Prophet*, 202–3).

57. "Howard Thurman Collection" at Boston University, http://hgar-srv3 .bu.edu/web/howard-thurman/howard-thurman-collection.

58. Howard Thurman, *Mysticism and Social Action* (London: International Association for Religious Freedom, 2014), Kindle location 371 of 1080.

59. Howard Thurman, *Footprints of a Dream: The Story of the Church for the Fellowship of All Peoples* (Eugene, OR: Wipf & Stock, 2009), 16.

60. "Rufus Jones," *Quaker Religious Thought* 46 (1978): 1–7.

61. Smith, *The Mystic as Prophet*, 167.

62. Robert G. Collmer, "The Limitations of Mysticism," *Bibliotheca Sacra* 116 (April 1959): 130–31.

63. Margaret Smith, *The Way of Mystics: The Early Christian Mystics and the Rise of the Sufis* (New York: Oxford University Press), 1978.

64. Personal email correspondence with Barbara Brown Taylor differentiating mental illness (specifically psychosis) from mystical experience (June 9, 2017).

65. Luther E. Smith, *Howard Thurman: The Mystic as Prophet* (Richmond, IN: Friends United Press, 1991), 34–35.

66. Drawing from the work of New Testament scholar Brian K. Blount, I conceive of the kingdom of God as "a transcendent space created through human action and divine intervention. When these forces align, the future kingdom forcibly and miraculously pierces into the present moment to overturn oppressions of the present age. Blount calls these kingdom inbreaking moments that alter time 'pockets of resistance.'" For additional information on how I expand this definition, see Gregory C. Ellison II, *Cut Dead but Still Alive: Caring for African American Men* (Nashville: Abingdon Press, 2013), 66–70. Also see Brian K. Blount, *Go Preach! Mark's Kingdom Message and the Black Church Today* (Maryknoll, NY: Orbis Books, 1998), 13–18, 68.

67. Thurman, *Mysticism and Social Action,* Kindle location 114 of 1080, 12 percent.

68. Ibid., Kindle location 335 of 1080, 31 percent.

69. Ibid., Kindle location 272 of 1080, 26 percent.

70. Thurman, *Deep Is the Hunger,* 62.

71. Smith, *The Mystic as Prophet,* 16–17.

72. Thurman, *Deep Is the Hunger,* 73–75.

73. Howard Thurman, "Those Who Walked with God," in *The Living Wisdom of Howard Thurman: A Visionary of Our Time* (Louisville, CO: Sounds True, 2010), audio recording.

74. Gregory C. Ellison II, *Cut Dead but Still Alive: Caring for African American Young Men* (Nashville: Abingdon Press, 2013), 82.

75. Ibid., 83.

76. Ibid., 79–80.

Index

achieved attributes, 93–94
activism, 123–30, 136, 139, 147
affinity, 91–92
African American young men, invisibility of, 74. *See also* Uth Turn
Agnew, Robert, 72
Altar in the World, An (Taylor), 29–31
Ambrose, Nancy, 132, 134
Angelou, Maya, 144
animators, 5
  beholding and, 50
  as Intimate Strangers, 56
  journey of, 62
  modeling vulnerability, 105–6
  as museum curators, 26–27
  prayers of, 23
  presence of, 22
  Radical Hospitality of, 23
  tools of, 9, 19–20, 31–32
  trust in, 23–24
anxiety, 101
apathy, 122, 134, 135, 139, 149, 150, 151, 162n30
Armah, Ayi Kwei, 29
ascribed attributes, 93–94
assimilation, 137

beholding, 40, 49–50
belonging, 77, 78
Bethune, Mary McLeod, 134
Big Boi, 33
Big Three. *See* apathy; despair; shame
Black Lives Matter, 90, 124, 127
Blount, Brian K., 163n66

Blum, Harold P., 154n2, 154n4, 155n7
Brooks, Gwendolyn, 144
Brown, Michael, 123–24, 126
Burghardt, Walter J., 95–96

Capps, Donald, 73, 122, 158nn5–6
Carmichael, Stokely, 127
cave art, 18–19, 21, 154nn2–4, 155n7
CeaseFire, 149, 150
centered speech, 105
change, 13
child development, 44–45
childhood
  imagination of, 24–26
  return to, 25, 26
  sensory immersion of, 25–26
Christ, symbol of, 122. *See also* Jesus
Christianity, Thurman's commitment to, 135–36
circles of trust, 103–6
closed questions, 108–9
common ground, reality of, 41
contemplation, 95, 111
control, 77, 79
conversation, fears regarding, 10
country dark, 15–16
Courage to Teach, The (Palmer), 108
crucibles, 54–55
cut dead, 67, 74–75, 78, 79, 99
Cut Dead but Still Alive: Caring for African American Young Men (Ellison), 2, 74, 149

165

Fearless Dialogues is far more than the words you have read in these pages. Fearless Dialogues is a grassroots organization led by a team of educators, artists, activists, connectors, and healers—we call them animators. These animators, who are trained in the signature Fearless Dialogues methodology, are uniquely skilled at creating spaces for hard, heartfelt conversations between unlikely partners. For information on how to bring trained animators from the Fearless Dialogues team to your community, church, or company, please go to www.fearless dialogues.com.

CPSIA information can be obtained
at www.ICGtesting.com
Printed in the USA
FFOW02n1557060118
44380217-44115FF

9 780664 260651